WHY I BELIEVE IN A PERSONAL GOD

The Credibility of Faith in a Doubting Culture

GEORGE CAREY
Archbishop of Canterbury

Harold Shaw Publishers
Wheaton, IL

First Published in Great Britain by Fount Paperbacks, London in 1989. This edition published in 1991 by special arrangement with Collins Publishers, 8 Grafton Street, London W1X 3LA England.

ISBN 0-87788-947-3

Library of Congress Cataloging-in-Publication Data

Carey, George.
    Why I believe in a personal God : the credibility of faith
  in a doubting culture / George Carey.
      p.   cm.
  Includes bibliographical references.
  ISBN 0-87788-947-3
  1. God.   2. Apologetics—20th century. I. Title.
BT102.C32   1991
231—dc20   90-23717
                                   CIP

---

99 98 97 96 95 94 93 92 91

10 9 8 7 6 5 4 3 2

Contents

Introduction

THAT GOD IS NEWS IS SOMETHING WE ALL KNOW. HE SEEMS TO pop up all the time—in our newspapers, in politics, and in daily life. Yet curiously enough for many in Western culture, he is the great irrelevance in our lives. Why is this? On the one hand, the case for the existence of God is strong; there are many intelligent people who do not find the idea of a personal God at all at odds with their knowledge of the world and universe. Indeed, they find him the integrating factor in human experience and knowledge. We might conclude from this that all that remains is for those who believe to convince those who do not. The problem is, I argue, that our Western culture has done us a serious disservice—it has so robbed us of the sense of the transcendent that we are unable to give due attention to the question of God. Our world is a one-dimensional gray world bereft of mystery, awe, and wonder.

It is not surprising therefore that we find ourselves scoffing at those with strong beliefs, yet wistfully envying their certainties and convictions. I hope then that this small book, written in the context of an extremely busy life, and probably showing all the marks of it, will be a help to those who thoughtfully return to the big question again: *Is there a God?* And if there is, how can we make contact with him?

For the sake of the general reader I have deliberately departed from the convention of footnotes. At the end of the book I have appended some of my sources and made suggestions for further reading. I trust that this decision will be of assistance to the person who simply wants to read the text and does not want to be told the number of books the author has press-ganged into his service!

I want to express my appreciation to all those who made this book possible. I am grateful for the Hockerill Educational Trust, who made it possible for me to study at Tanture Ecumenical Institute in Jerusalem where most of the preparatory work was done; and for my son, Andrew, who read over the manuscript and made some constructive remarks and saved me from some amusing howlers. I take the blame for any he did not spot!

1

The Great "God" Robbery

THE 64,000 DOLLAR QUESTION IS NOT, "CAN YOU LEND ME 64,000 dollars?" but "Is there a God?" That is, can modern intelligent men and women *seriously* accept rationally that there is a divine creator of this mysterious and fascinating universe who loves us and wants to enter into a relationship with us? There is no denying the urgency of such a question because the future as well as the credibility of Christianity rests upon the answer we give. How can we preach that Jesus Christ is the answer to our needs if there is a major question concerning the existence of the Father to whom he pointed? I know of many people who are attracted to the person of Christ but who raise fundamental questions about God* him-

*We talk about God as "he" but must appreciate that such language is only analogical. God is "wholly other." For more on this see p. 116.

self. They look at the world and their experience of it and say: "I see much that makes me disbelieve in such a divine being—the inexplicable tragedies that happen to others, the random nature of things that does not suggest a Planner, the cruelty and rapaciousness of nature. Can a kind, benevolent creator be behind such a place as this?"

This book is written to tackle such questions directly and honestly. I do so because I too have had to wrestle with them and still do. If it is any comfort to others, I have never found it easy to believe in God. Even though I am the Archbishop of Canterbury, honesty requires me to say that my search for God and my finding of him have not been simple or painless. There have been times of great agonizing doubt but I have never lost sight of the need to come to a decision on this important issue. *If* there is a God who can be known and experienced, then the consequences for us are exciting indeed. They will affect our personal lives and behavior as well as our corporate experience. If there is no personal God behind the things that are, we must equally face up to the implications of living in a universe in which there is only ultimate futility and purposelessness. This does not negate what happiness or meaning we may care to thrust into life, but it would signify that all of life is on a slide that takes us down to blackness and nothingness. The consequences of this belief affect all we are and what we do.

My own investigations over a period of many years have given me a quiet assurance that there is a God who has given us sufficient clues in life, nature, human thought, beauty, and art to satisfy the genuine inquirer that he exists, and that he has expressed himself most meaningfully in Jesus Christ. However, you may come to a different conclusion at the end of this study, and that is your right as a thinking, responsible person. All I can do is invite you to join me in looking at the arguments again, to consider whether you agree that there are sufficient reasons for us to believe in a "divine" being who is "out there" as well as "with us"—a "Being" who has created the universe and still pours his creativity into it. I would like to think that, as well as the thinking inquirer who may read this book, it will be of help to Christians who just want to be reminded of the great truths of the Christian faith. I hope it will encourage you and make you more confident as a Christian today.

But before we get to work there is one fact we must face up to—the skepticism of Western society when it comes to believing in God. Such skepticism is not the result of honest reflection and argument that has led to agnosticism but rather the opposite—unthinking conclusions that emanate from assumptions current in our society. This came home to me with great force when I was once interviewing a young prisoner. When I mentioned God, he scoffed and said, "Well, nobody believes in God these days, do they!" I asked him to give me one good reason why I should not and he fell silent in helpless confusion, unable to give one coherent thought to back up his remark. What he was doing, actually, was expressing an attitude, not an argument. He is not alone. Western society, through its ceaseless search for materialistic prosperity, has created a climate that makes it difficult for us to comprehend the supernatural. Agnosticism has been pres-

ent in all cultures since mankind started to think about ultimate questions, but what is totally novel is the fact of agnostic
culture itself, which creates a climate of unbelief insidious in
its effects and consequences. So, for the genuine inquirer or
believer, it feels like running up an escalator that is coming
down because the assumptions of our society are naturalistic,
and this worldly and dismissive of ideas does not "ring cash
registers," "build houses," or result in something "practical."
God has been marginalized, not by thought or argument, but
by the consequences of pragmatic attitudes to life that have
had their effect in every area of human living.

In short we have become conceptual "Philistines." We have
moved away from the really big questions such as Kant's great
trio of questions that concluded his *Critique of Pure Reason*:
What can I know? What ought I to do? What may I hope for?
Instead, the whole sweep of creative conceptual thinking
outlined in Kant's questions, which I believe stands behind
human nature as moral, spiritual, and eternal, has been shattered into a million fragments, reducing the life and destiny
of humankind to an unattractive, gray materialism.

This is not, indeed, to deny the rich contribution that
science, and technology in particular, have made to human
progress. None of us wishes to return to a past, void of the
fruits of scientific achievement. We all recognize that the last
hundred years have seen a revolution in the history of humankind and we are generally thankful for it. What I am pointing
out is the loss of the great ideological questions. Unless you
are a religious person, or perhaps someone with a strong
ideology, you will not have anything greater than yourself to

believe in. No longer dwarfed by questions about the transcendent, no longer awed and thrilled by the wonder of creation, we have settled for an attitude to life that is basically functional and materialistic. The message fed to us from birth is that there are no transcendent questions to bother about. Rather, the really important issues concern this life: our standard of living, our professional careers, the education of our children, and so on. So, we live in an age in which the divine, at least in its classical forms, has receded into the background of human concerns and consciousness. We have been robbed of God not by coming to such a conclusion after careful, considered, reflective thought but by acquired attitudes, assumptions, and transferred values of a culture that is conditioning us not to believe.

Three important aspects of this robbing need to be noted. First, there is the *separation* of the individual from his or her community. We are told repeatedly that one of the glories of Western civilization is the place given to the individual person, resulting in greater freedom of choice and opportunities for personal fulfillment. While I have no wish to deny the obvious benefits of our civilization we have to point out the negative elements within the process of individuation. Take the claim that we have greater freedom to choose. Is this the case? It seems otherwise when we begin to analyze the situation. The process of modern life has led to the weakening of the all-embracing and all-sustaining communities of pre-Industrial society. Modern people are now more mobile, more anonymous, free to belong to and to choose what kind of society they wish to identify with. But the paradox is that,

at the same time, the sophistication of modern life has led to the
replacement of the communities that used to have such influence over the individual by abstract megastructures, are more
anonymous and controlling than anything that preceded them.
The "global village" of the modern world means that, un-
beknown to most of us, our lives, our leisure, our patterns of
eating and drinking, and the values we cherish are influenced
most profoundly by forces beyond ourselves. The irony, therefore, is that it has led to less freedom of choice. A clear example
of this in the country where I reside, present-day Britain, is in
the media, which used to be proudly extolled as an example of
a free and independent source of communication. Few would
claim that nowadays. As a diocesan bishop, and therefore a little
closer to the center of news distribution than I used to be, I have
become alarmed by the way the public is controlled, protected,
and even sometimes manipulated by those who have such
power over the media. It is inevitable, then, that our beliefs about
life and death and our value judgments are going to be shaped
by what we read and see.

Then there is the process of *secularization*, which is the
consequence of many complex factors that include the impact of industrialization, the Enlightenment, and the failure of
the churches to communicate the essence of Christianity.
Without the individual being consciously aware of it, this
movement constitutes a massive threat to an appreciation of
the transcendent in human existence. Now, what do we mean
by "secularization"? I mean by this term a process of change
within society, either deliberate or unconscious, that leaves

God out, electing for the material in preference to the
spiritual, the worldly over and against eternal values. The
process of secularization appears complete when supernatural faith becomes private and optional. In many developed countries this process appears almost complete, but the
result is serious for the individual and community. It is not
only religious thinkers who recognize that secularization
frustrates deeply grounded aspirations in the heart of the
average man and woman whose natural desire is to belong
and to exist in a meaningful, friendly, and hopeful universe.
Indeed, the poet Philip Larkin in his verse "Church Going"
points out the dilemma left for modern people:

> When churches fall completely out of use
> What shall we turn them into . . .
> . . . superstition, like belief must die
> and what remains when disbelief has gone?
> Grass, weedy pavements, brambles, buttress, sky,
> A shape less recognisable every week,
> A purpose more obscure.

Yet even for this humanist poet the church meant something:

> A serious house on serious earth it is,
> In whose blent air all our compulsions meet,
> Are recognised, and robed as destinies.
> And that much never can be obsolete,

Since someone will forever be surprising
A hunger in himself to be more serious . . .

Then there is the third aspect in modern life that is a
consequence of secularization, namely, a *pluralism of value
structures*. Most developed nations now display a pluralism
of values, ideologies, and beliefs that would have been un-
thinkable two decades ago. Go to any town or big city and it
will exhibit all the aspects of a United Nations with every
conceivable faith expressed in its life. No doubt this gives a
richness and excitement that adds a great deal to the quality
of life but it is not without its drawbacks also. The fundamental problem is that no longer is there to be found a coherent
value system that the majority affirm and recognize.

Some years ago, when I was vicar of St. Nicholas' Durham,
I was approached by a lecturer at the University and his wife
who wished to enroll their children in Sunday school and to
attend church, even though they themselves were agnostics.
"Why," I asked, "do you want your children to hear the
Christian message when you yourselves have rejected it?"
Their reply intrigued and impressed me. They complained
about the lack of standards in modern society and affirmed
the importance of values and then said, "We want our children
to grow up in a big 'story'; a story that will give them security,
meaning, and a hope. It will be their decision later to accept
or reject it, but if we do not encourage them to know the
Christian 'story,' they will never be able to understand what
it is they have rejected." This couple went on to express their
gratitude for the central role of the Christian story in express-

ing Christian values as well as forming the marvelous cultural and literary traditions that are central to European and North American culture. "We don't want diminished children," they concluded.

We could easily assume that this gloomy analysis of modern life in the preceding paragraphs indicates that Western civilization is irredeemably materialistic and atheistic. However, I am not arguing that. What I am suggesting is that our assumptions are materialistic and un-spiritual with the net result that reflections about God and the claims of Jesus Christ have little chance of being considered seriously. The irony, however, is that modern people are not totally devoid of interest in the supernatural. Indeed not. Somehow this aspect of the human spirit rises to the surface in all kinds of ways. At its most basic level we know of many in our society who, though they do not attend church regularly, believe in God, pray devoutly, and seem to have a deep awareness of the transcendent. This dimension is not despised or ignored. The behavior of the many thousands who visit cathedrals and churches all over the world as tourists shows that many of them have a residual faith that is stirred by the "signals of the transcendent," which they find in such places.

But then there is the presence in modern society of those who dabble in the occult or astrology, who watch for UFOs, contact spirits, follow the tenets of scientology and other strange groups, practice transcendental meditation, and so on. All this testifies to the continued pervasiveness of religion. However, most thinking people are put off by the uncritical and superstitious bases of such movements and trends. Nevertheless, the fact of their existence is significant. The American novelist Saul Bellow makes one of his characters say in *Herzog*: "People are dying—it is no metaphor—for lack of something real to carry home when the day is done. See how willingly they accept the wildest nonsense."

Then, of course, there are quasi-religious instincts in us that overlap with faith, and that might coincide with what Philip Larkin meant by being serious about our destinies and compulsions. We can think of art, music, drama, and literature that point beyond the mundane and thus feed the souls of people. Often, although not always, the appeal of aesthetics can substitute for what the Christian calls spirituality.

We must also note at civic and national levels the instinctive need felt by authorities to interpret significant events—tragedies, celebrations—religiously. While it is true that churchgoing has declined in recent years in Britain, the interest in the church has not. The Church of England has never enjoyed so much media attention as it has received over the last five years. While there are particular reasons for this attention, the fact remains that as Western culture has become secularized the issue of faith stubbornly refuses to go away.

First, it refuses to go away at the *corporate* level. Eisenhower once remarked: "Our government makes no sense unless it is founded in a deeply religious faith—and I don't care what it is!" While that possibly says a great deal about Eisenhower's lack of interest in the character of a faith, he was rightly giving expression to a deep-seated feeling in most of us that if society's values and morality do not spring from an eternal source, that society will be impoverished. The Jewish theologian, J. Neusner, once remarked that "The sense of the transcendent is the heart of culture, the very essence of humanity. A civilisation that is devoted exclusively to the utilitarian is at bottom not different from barbarianism. The world is sustained by unworldliness." We might as well say that our God-idea is the acid test of our valuation of life.

Second, it refuses to go away at the *personal* level. Peter Berger observes in one of his books the resurgence of religion in quarters where one would least expect it and he puts it down to the inability of secular world views to answer the deeper questions of the human condition; questions of whence, whither, and why that are ineradicably linked with personhood. He speaks of the "pervasive boredom of a world without gods."

It is crucial then that we start with this background. Unless you and I realize that the world view we have inherited has made us biased against questions about the supernatural we will not be able to consider the issue of God in a fair-minded way. Without any ques... ...n robbed of

Go... ...world view

ma... ...mensional

vie... ...ur hearts.

Ho... ...ity, many

are... ...e of them

into... ...perience

and t... ...aped us.

Many... ...ith.

2

The Case against God

IN THE LAST CHAPTER I WAS SUGGESTING THAT THE CLIMATE OF modern life has created an atmosphere that has made it very difficult, if not embarrassing, to talk about God in a meaningful way. Talk about politics, sports, or current affairs, and there will be spirited discussion with people who are quick to make their positions known. But talk about God— and there is often a hushed and uncomfortable silence. Of course, we allow him a place in our jokes, and even in important national ceremonies. Religion, it seems, is not a fit topic for civilized people, although curiously most people find it important to give it a significant role in dignifying our most solemn ceremonies at private and public moments.

But, to be fair, we cannot attribute the problem completely to modern disregard for matters of faith. The problem is partly created by the facts themselves. Our own experience, as well as the experience of many others, confronts us with serious challenges to the existence of God and forces us to ask, "Is it really possible for intelligent people to believe that a divine, personal Force is responsible for this universe? Is belief in God the final mythology that must go?"

Let us take four issues that are at the heart of modern people's dilemma. For many intelligent people, the central problem revolves around our interpretation of life and our experience of it. Two particular issues emerge from this. First, the model of the universe we have inherited is one that comes without a theistic context or theistic values. So, for example, at the level of world history we have imbibed a picture of life as the product of vast impersonal forces that go back millions of years. Countless millions of species have been spawned by an over-generous, even profligate, Nature to fill the world as we know it, and in the ensuing history of evolution the weakest and least adaptable forms of life have perished. Entire species have passed away whereas other forms of life have appeared that are destructive and harmful. There may be elements of purpose on a random scale as we look at the whole but there does not seem to be a very caring Providence at work. Thus a new picture of the physical universe and the place of humanity within it has replaced the old cosmology of God at the center with humanity as his co-regent and partner. And as this picture of life has permeated the corporate mentality of Western people, the pattern of our thought has changed with the result that our concept of life, on the whole, is not that of Providence watching over us but is that of an indifferent and uncaring universe that we have to conquer and bring under control.

Along with this assumption, our experience of life either directly, or indirectly through the experiences of others, sometimes leads us to assume that life itself is better explained on the assumption that there is no God rather than that God exists and cares. Where is God, people say, when thousands die suddenly in a volcanic disaster or are swept away in a flood? For some Jews the experience of Auschwitz shattered the concept of a merciful God who cares for his people. The Jewish writer Richard Rubenstein asks, "How can a Jew believe in an omnipotent beneficent God after Auschwitz?" The experience of such evil, he felt, was so overwhelmingly horrible that the whole idea of God had to be revised. We acknowledge that this was not by any means the total Jewish experience, because there were many other Jews who did not believe that the character of man's sin should form the agenda for believing in God or not. Nevertheless, even for such devout Jews the question that the Second World War focussed so sharply was, "In the light of such atrocities—where is God?" Thus, the lonely experience of their people during the dark days of the war brought about a major rethinking in the Jewish understanding of God.

Although such awful events are outside the experience of most of us, we are all aware of the character of human tragedy. We are confronted by it daily as our television sets bring it unannounced into our living rooms. The danger is that this medium can trivialize or even treat it as another element of entertainment. For example, in a recent earthquake in Mexico the television cameras showed the horrifying picture of a trapped little girl of eight who could not be freed from her prison. We could see her head and hear her cries and her prayers—and we heard her die. While it may not have been the intention of the television producer to bring us anything other than news of that awful incident, the superficial quality of the item, programmed to give us instant information, is an example of a tendency to sensationalize rather than inform.

Of course, there is nothing new in this. We are used to reading about tragedy or seeing it happen to others. When, however, it actually happens to us, it ceases to be external and academic and takes on a personal shape. When tragedy hits our own family unit or that of friends, and we have to make sense of the apparently futile happening striking those nearest and dearest to us, we find ourselves asking: Where is God when our child is run over or has leukemia? What kind of god is it who allows these things to happen to us? If he cannot intervene in life when such things happen and when prayer does not seem to work, does it not make more sense to abandon belief in God completely and accept the fact that we are living in a world that is bereft of a loving God, bereft of purpose and meaning? But, as we shall see later, this conclusion is not inevitable. Somehow belief in a God who cares cannot be shrugged off that easily, the problem of good has to be set against the problem of evil, purposeful events in life against random happenings, morality against immorality, and design against chaos. Nevertheless, the problem of pain and evil remains as the greatest obstacle facing the person who sincerely wants to be a believer. Yet, we have to ask, how much of this problem goes back to a mindset that has already assumed that God is absent?

A second problem that faces the outsider is that no one these days pretends that we can prove the existence of God from logical argument. Lord Boothby once described God as "that being who exists to have his being proved and disproved," and so it might seem from the development of Christian dogma, which has tried to convince people by argument that reason can lead them to God. Take the famous *cosmological argument* so beloved by Thomas Aquinas. This argument is one that depends upon a link between cause and effect. As Thomas saw it, everything must have a cause; everything in life comes from potentiality to actuality. Furthermore, there must be a profound similarity between cause and effect; that is, the effect cannot be greater than the cause. Thomas's argument tried to prove that we are led by logic back to a Great Unmoved Mover who was the originating cause of all things. But, philosophically considered, this argument, cogent as it may seem, has two major fallacies. To begin with, why stop at a First Cause? It seems very plausible at first sight that we might be able to trace all of reality back to one Uncaused Event—namely, God himself. But—why stop at all? Why should there not be an infinite regress of causes and effects?

Then again, Thomas Aquinas argues that the effect cannot be greater than the cause. It is clearly not the case that a cause *has* to be equal to its effects. We know from experience that often something profoundly superior may proceed from the inferior and the history of evolution is an overwhelming testimony to this, proving that the greater does come from the lesser.

The other "proofs" have not fared any better. The argument from design seems at first sight to be very convincing. We see all around us evidence of purpose in creation—that delicate flower, that piece of machinery, the order and rhythm of life—all this and more suggests not a chaotic world but one deliberately planned by a creator. Archdeacon Paley in the last century made this argument famous with his analogy of the world as a clock and God as a purposeful clockmaker who designed an intricate machine and left it to tick away. But as we saw earlier the analogy clearly fails. There is certainly evidence of order and purpose but this does not necessarily indicate that it is the work of a loving Providence. If the world is a clock it certainly does not function as one because there is nothing predictable about the world as a whole or human existence in particular. Disorder flourishes alongside order, the order of cancer creating a world of disorder.

The failure to find a completely convincing argument for God's existence after two thousand years of trying may suggest that it is time to abandon the attempt, throw in the towel, and concede that we have made God in our image. God is dead. But Christians are confident that this obituary notice has gone in too early because the idea of God is too persistent to go the way of the Greek mythologies. We shall be returning to the question of proofs, or "clues" as I prefer to call them, later, but two things can be said immediately to the cry, "Let's abandon faith in God." First, logical proof is necessarily limited to a range of things where the answer is already included in the data. We call this *a priori* reasoning because the argument proceeds from data before us. For example, the answer to 144 multiplied by 145 is deduction from what is already implicit in numbers. *A priori* reasoning has a most important place in life, especially where mathematics form the basis of science. But how limited this pathway of knowledge really is, in spite of its importance. Just think how splendid it would be if the most complex questions of life could be solved that simply. Think of political issues to do with human freedom, economic justice, male/female and black/white relationships. How convenient it would be if everyone could agree about the conclusion to be reached! But experience shows that life does not come in that form and shape and most of our genuine "knowing" has more than just a whiff of speculation about it.

A personal illustration might help to bring this home. After twenty-eight years of happy marriage to a truly magnificent person who has fulfilled all the hopes I have rested in her, I still cannot prove that she loves me. I have plenty of clues, of course, but no direct, tangible proof that would satisfy the objective outsider who, perhaps, had to make up his mind in a few hours. Suppose in that brief period he caught us having an argument! Would that not act as a serious objection to the flimsy statement that "she loves me"? Again, even in the best of relationships there have been the bad moments, the times when cruel things have been said and mischief planned. Do we not have to take these into the reckoning? Yes, indeed, we must and they are important clues concerning the nature of human knowing because love grows from disappointment and conflict. Love cannot be proved because there is always a great open-endedness about it and to say "she loves me" implies a strong element of faith. That does not mean that one cannot say "she loves me." Indeed, we can say that and much more; that this kind of love is far superior to any form of love that can be proved by deductive reasoning, because of necessity that which is measurable is bound to be superficial and very limited, whereas the experience of love forged over many years will deepen and continue to grow forever. So Professor J. Baillie comments: "A high degree of probability is the most that can be claimed for any scientific result. Yet, the strange fact is that I have more confidence in what common sense and pre-scientific experience tell me about my natural environment than in any of the things I have learned from science. I have, for example, a greater degree of assurance of the honesty and loyalty of some of my friends than I have of the validity of any scientific doctrine and still more secure is my conviction that honesty and loyalty are things required of us."

The second observation is that attempting to prove God says a great deal about our concept of God and our understanding of ourselves. We make him into an element of knowledge "out there" and our implicit thinking is that "if only we had the right receiving equipment we could hear him speaking to us." I have no wish to deny the fact that God is outside of us in a real sense, but such space-time concepts are manifestly anthropocentric. In a profound way, we have to realize that if there is a God, we are "inside" him. He is not "out there" as if he is a statistic, fact, or piece of knowledge. Rather, if he is the God of Christian theology, he is the whole of knowledge—and he will therefore be ultimately beyond knowledge unless he chooses to reveal himself. Because of him, it is possible for knowing and knowledge to exist.

But for the moment we must stay with the fact that the Christian church has given up the attempt to prove the existence of God. He cannot be measured or confined according to the patterns of our ways.

A third objection to God is closely linked with the problem of meaning. When Christians talk about God, surely, we might think, their words should have the same meaning as when they are used in day-by-day life. Here we meet the problem of logic and common-sense meanings. Centuries ago Augustine focussed upon the problem when he posed that the presence of evil in the world implies that either God is good and yet limited in some way, or that he is powerful but not good. It seemed to Augustine in his pre-Christian days that God could not be both. In theological language this meant that his omnipotence and his beneficence were in conflict. If he were good and powerful, then it seemed that he would intervene on behalf of the poor and helpless. The fact that he doesn't seems to indicate that we have to make a choice. Of course, as Augustine was to see later as a Christian, there are factors that we have to take into account that diminish this actual problem. For example, perhaps God has a plan that takes into account all the world's sufferings and evils. Again, the simple either/or approach may be making the assumption that it is this world's cares that matter. But if God has prepared for those who love him such a wealth of joy and happiness that dwarfs the brief and transitory pains of earth (no matter how awful they may seem to us) does not this put the whole issue in a completely different context? In other words, when we talk in terms of either omnipotence or goodness but not both, we are smuggling in a value system with its own built-in assumption that if God exists, he must exist to make us all happy in this life.

However, although we have to be very cautious when we use this argument, we have to acknowledge that if words mean anything at all it is sometimes very difficult to talk about God being good when things happen that contradict our understanding of what a good friend would do for us. For example, if I tell a young lady that she is beautiful, graceful, and intelligent and in the same breath add, "but it is a pity you are so awkward, a little dense and 100 pounds overweight"— she will be very puzzled, as well as very annoyed! The point is that the additional statement has shattered the earlier idea with which we started. Now, of course, this is obvious when we use ordinary language, but if words are to carry their normal values we become aware of the problems when we speak about God as good. At the moment of writing this chapter I am dealing with an intelligent couple whose eleven-year-old son died very inexplicably during a sports afternoon at school. They have no church connections whatever. So how do I interpret for them the activity of God in this situation? How can I tell them that in spite of what they are experiencing, God actually loves them and cares for them and he has taken their son to himself? Now I happen to believe that is the case, but my confidence rests on many years of working things out theologically as a Christian. It is not possible that those outside the Christian family can see it in the same way, because it is clearly not good for them.

Thus the Christian or any theist struggles with language when she is trying to convey something of the meaning of God for others. Christian thinkers find help in referring to analogy when we talk about God. It is clear, for example, that when we try to talk about any deep reality that is beyond space or time that we will be forced into metaphors, pictures, and analogies. Listen to Gerard Hopkins trying to convey something of the splendor of creation:

The world is charged with the grandeur of God
It will shine forth as shining from shook foil

Watch any film of a literary masterpiece and you will see the inability of the screen to express real emotion or the depth of human expression. Some things are beyond words and we hopelessly resort to pictures. Science itself is not immune from this. Popularizers of science have not hesitated to use diagrams, metaphors, and concepts to portray realities that are beyond the reach of human words. Indeed, modern quantum physicists are not afraid to use metaphor and poetry to describe the realities that are their concern.

A fourth problem for the sincere person who would like to believe but finds it difficult is located in the idea of belief itself. Such a person might put it this way: "I'd actually like to believe but find the whole concept of worship rather puzzling. I don't think I need God to find my way in life. I cope very well, I enjoy the finer things of life, beauty, art, and music, and find genuine pleasure in these things. Frankly, church bores me. It is not that I hate the service, the people, or even the vicar! It is just that it is not for me." I think we have to heed this kind of statement very seriously. There are people who, to quote Karl Rahner, are "unmusical in religion." That is to say, those who do not appear to pick up the sounds that other people hear and we have to admit that there are plenty of them around—in our family circles, at work, and among our friends. For such people who appear to get by happily without the God hypothesis, what has faith to say to them? Is God only useful as a support for church attendance and for those who conform to the practices of established religion? I only hope that those who are "unmusical" in such matters to do with organized Christianity will be concerned with the central matter of belief. If our inquiry leads us to the con- clusion that God exists and has appeared in and through the ministry of Jesus Christ, the logic will lead us on to doing something about it.

For some, like Erich Fromm, the great psychiatrist, the problem is linked with the thrust of a faith. He criticizes

Christianity in particular because it appears to address its message mainly to weak people. He agrees that it is very successful in helping the weak and needy but he asserts that if it is to be successful in the modern world it must have a message for strong people, those who do not have problems, people who are successful in life and who can cope. What, asks Fromm, is your message to people like me who are happy, contented, and balanced? Bonhoeffer, of course, addressed a similar question before his untimely death. The world has come of age, he thought, and does not need the religion of former times. How can the church minister in a religionless age? What is its message to those who not only appear not to need it but actually despise it?

But a curious illogicality runs through this argument. What has need to do with it? We all recognize that there are those who do not feel any particular religious need. Perhaps most of us are like that and this is a question that we shall return to later. And Fromm's argument that Christianity is more attractive to weak than to strong people is certainly highly contentious! More people choose not to go to church because they have other interests than because they have logically come to the conclusion that God does not exist. Need is *not* the issue—truth is. If God *is,* then our unmusicality in religion is neither here nor there. If he is the Lord of the universe, then I stand before him as a child of the universe and must work out what this relationship now means and what I must do about it.

3

Is the Universe on Our Side?

A VERY INTERESTING SHIFT IN OUR THINKING HAS TAKEN place since man set foot on the moon. Although Copernicus, years ago, destroyed the idea that the sun and stars revolve around the earth, an earth-bound approach to life was practically impossible to shift because our experience of life was confined to the limits of our knowledge here. But since 1969 a wholly new consciousness of the universe has begun to filter into the experience of us all; as a result, we have begun to be conscious of our place in the universe and not merely in our world. We are now used to seeing the earth from satellite pictures with the vast spaces of the universe behind. Furthermore, the signals being transmitted to us from our space ships, interviewing the nearest planets, increase our new sense of awareness of being children of a universe that dwarfs our tiny world.

Now, how do we react to this? Our response can take one of two main forms. First, we may be excited and awed by this realization. We now know so much more about the universe than before and its very size frankly makes comprehension of it extremely difficult. How can we possibly absorb the fact that, as far as we can tell, the universe consists of innumerable galaxies like our own; the nearest one to us being 900,000 light years away! Yet, although we are dwarfed by the immensity of all that is, the nature of our humanity comes out in our desire to understand and inhabit the cold confines of limitless space. We want to know and we respond eagerly to the challenge. We project our thoughts beyond ourselves and ask whether perhaps there are other species like us out there inhabiting worlds similar to our own. Is it conceivable that we are a unique offshoot of Mother Nature? Is ours the only world in the entire universe where there is conscious life?

A common assumption today is that our planet cannot be unique; there must exist somewhere in the universe sentient, thinking beings with whom we shall eventually make contact. But at the moment this remains a matter of faith because no evidence whatsoever has come to light to substantiate that theory, only the odds that we cannot be a freak. Given similar conditions in a similar world, it is likely, so we are told, that similar beings exist somewhere. This conclusion I have no wish to dispute. That may well be so. Given the disastrous mess that humanity has made of God's world it is at least possible that God could be trying other experiments elsewhere! What we cannot doubt, however, is that our new sense of the universe has challenged our thinking concerning the nature of God himself. No longer is it possible to think of God in domestic terms. He is, if he exists, a being who cannot be adequately caught by the workings of the human mind, who is wholly other and only knowable in so far as he reveals himself to us.

A second response, beside that of awe, which leads to intellectual curiosity, is that of sheer metaphysical numbness when one begins to comprehend the nature of the universe. Here is the start of existential doubt. Consider the psychological effect of this piece of information. We are told that the light from the cluster of galaxies in Hydra that reaches us has traveled through space for two thousand million light years. That cluster is only one of the innumerable galaxies, each made up of millions of stars, separated from each other by immeasurable stretches of inter-galactic space. Ponder this picture of the universe and then ask: "What do I mean when I say God?" How much closer seems the domestic God of the Bible who made the heavens and the earth! The size of the universe tends to terrify us and seems to place beyond our reach a God who cares. We find ourselves thinking: "All this is so vast that if there is a God, he cannot possibly be interested in the antics of a tiny species on a third-rate planet orbiting a tenth-rate sun." It is against this realistic background

laws. Once we begin to think about it, it must strike us all as an astonishing fact. We took it all for granted at school. Our textbooks on physics, biology, and chemistry opened to us a world in which we are able to study the principles that govern the patterns of life and also predict how things behave.

The kind of order I am thinking of might be best illustrated by an analogy. Let us suppose a traveler, in visiting a foreign land, finds himself entering a deserted house in a wilderness. It strikes him that although there is no sign of the presence of another person, there are signs that someone has been there before him. He deduces this because everything in the house is sufficient for his survival. To be sure, not everything is ready-made or fully prepared, but all the ingredients are there, everything works in a clocklike way. So he concludes that the evidence of order indicates that the house has had an owner and it could be that he is still around. He could have come to another conclusion, of course. He might have decided that it only seems to suggest order, and the likeliest hypothesis is that it is an amazing coincidence to find in the wilderness a place of such convenience. He might also have concluded that in spite of many opportunities, the former occupant has never showed up, thus proving that the house was just a freak happening. However, the more order he finds in the house, discovering that he and his descendants are able to grow within it and never tire of new discoveries to meet the needs of new situations, the more he may come to see the hypothesis of it happening by chance as unconvincing.

We recognize the deficiency of all analogies, but I am suggesting that such striking implicit intelligence and temporal order forces us to give an account of it. Now when you and I use our technology in day-to-day working situations, we can adopt at least three different attitudes to such inherent rationality. The first is that we can take it all for granted. It is there. This is the most common attitude in our society. The fact that the world is rational neither proves the existence of God nor disproves it. Sadly, when we did science at school few of our teachers opened our eyes to the wonder of all around us. We were never taught to ask "Why?" but simply taught that "It exists" without any explanation given. But science without wonder leads to the impoverishment of the human spirit. This can result in a Philistine stance that exploits the goodness of life and does not apprehend the Goodness in life.

A second and probably more common attitude among thinking people, if asked to say something about the presence of rationality in the nature of things, would probably be that rationality is a concept we impose upon the world. "It simply is not the case that raw data is rational," says a sympathetic but agnostic friend. "All that we find in life are the building blocks of scientific discovery and when some order is found, we project back into the data the concept of rationality! If you are going on to say that this 'proves' the existence of God, it does nothing of the sort. All it shows is that you have made an unwarranted jump from 'Things make sense' to 'It is God who makes them sensible.' So our friend attempts to pour cold water upon the concept of the universe as basically intelligible. For him, rationality resides in us and not in the world around and its structures. All we are able to say is that

the character of the world is such that it has produced intelligent beings. Nothing more can or ought to be said than this.

I respond very seriously to the thrust of the last point. It is
very tempting for the Christian believer to say, "Didn't I tell
you that this proves the existence of God? Open your eyes
and see his handiwork all around us!" But this is not what I
am arguing. Instead I would assert that we can say a lot more
than that the character of the world just happens to have
produced sentient, intelligent beings. The point I am trying
to make as strongly as possible is that the element of intelligibility is not something that we impose on things after we
have created something, but it is already there in our environment as well as in ourselves. The world is either intelligible
or not; if it is not, science is impossible because the world
would be haphazard and chaotic. But that is not our experience; rather it is predictable and orderly. I am not arguing
that a mysterious purpose called "God" is somehow present
in that inanimate piece of steel that will eventually become a
car chassis or the wool that will become a skirt. Of course not.
But we are only able to make these things because there is a
basic irretrievable "givenness" about the world and our place
in it that has propelled humanity from a primitive home in the
seas or the trees (whichever theory of evolution one takes)
to the limitless possibilities that still exist before us—assuming
that our predilection to self-destruction does not lead to a final
act of total genocide.

The point I have just been making is that the world as it
is—with all the ready-made ingredients for intelligent life,
thus making possible the wonder of science, art, and human

growth and development—requires an explanation. Now it could be countered by someone saying, "Yes. I can see why a theist believes in God on this bases. I grant you that the order and signs of intelligence are there and this makes all our knowledge possible. But what if it all depends upon an initial act of complete random chance? What if the creation of the universe is but the inevitable outcome of a series of accidents at the beginning of time? If that were the case, we would not conclude that the order indicates the presence of intelligent activity on the part of a divine being we call 'God' but, rather, the order is but the manifestation of structural order that keeps the Cosmos going." Some have illustrated this by saying that although a monkey could not produce the complete words of Shakespeare, it is conceivable that three thousand monkeys typing for two thousand years would eventually yield this result at some point in time. This idea is as improbable as a similar sentiment expressed in the limerick:

There was once a hairy baboon
Who breathed down a bassoon.
For he said: "It appears,
in a billion years—
I shall certainly hit on a tune.

But this idea that instinctive reaction working itself out over millions of years can burst forth into brilliant creativity is most certainly nonsense. Irrationality cannot give rise to rationality in that kind of form. For the sake of argument let us accept the unlikely idea that haphazard blowings by a baboon may hit upon the *Trumpet Voluntary*, but even accepting that the law of averages states it might happen, such a mindless discovery of a tune falls a long way short of the rational, purposeful, creative mind that composed the tune in the first place.

If, then, we can say cautiously that it is reasonable to conclude that the impressive order in the universe might be the work of a personal Intelligence, we seem to be in a position to wonder whether there is any other evidence to believe in the existence of a creator.

Let us now go back to the problem of "Someone who started it all." This, actually, is our gut-reaction. You ask the average person and you will discover that most people find the cause and effect argument a reasonable ground for believing in God. "There must be a God who created all this" is a common assumption. This should not be dismissed as hopeful credulity because often it is said by people who are not practicing Christians at all. Many are students of life whose convictions stem not from analytical thinking in a study but from lifetime reflection on the character of life and the beauty of creation.

Nevertheless, as we have seen, the cause and effect argument is not without its difficulties. That d is the result of c, which is the result of b, which is the result of a, is all very obvious. But the statement that a is the beginning of the series requires an explanation. Why stop there? Is a the logical origin of b, thus causing c and d? If not, perhaps a itself is caused? This is the basic difficulty with the famous First Cause argument as propounded by Aquinas. We can happily accept that we can trace back the steps into the past, but why is it necessary to introduce God as the ultimate cause of all? Why not an infinite regress as was suggested earlier?

It seems then that the First Cause argument is badly holed by a logical flaw but, interestingly, this ancient argument has reappeared somewhat strengthened by two considerations. The first has to do with recent cosmological theories. It is now commonly believed that the universe had a beginning in time. As long as Hoyle's steady state theory prevailed, which argued that the universe has always existed in a state of perfect equilibrium, the First Cause argument was bound to be unfashionable. However, this theory has since given way to discoveries in radio astronomy that suggest that in one wholly inexplicable explosion the universe began its life. It has been possible to date the origin of the universe to an explosion that occurred about eighteen million years ago. Two particular arguments bolster the theory that the universe is finite. The first is the second law of thermodynamics which, as one of the universal laws of life, simply explains the process of life and death. Order is always followed by disorder, life by death. Scientists conclude from this that if, as is likely, the universe is moving towards its own decay and death, the conclusion is that it must be a finite universe and did not always exist. The second reason is that the American astronomer, Edwin Hubble, discovered that galaxies, instead of remaining in a stable condition, were in fact rushing apart. This discovery was to prove decisive. Radio astronomy has verified this hypothesis of the expanding universe, which again supports the idea of a universe that had a beginning in time. We are also told that all the ingredients for life were encoded within the first ten seconds of the beginning of the universe. Little wonder that Dr. Schwiama's lecture on the Origin of Life on Radio Three commenced with the announcer saying, "Professor Schwiama will not be saying anything about the supernatural beginnings of the universe as the natural beginnings are strange enough!"

It is important that we should not fall back into the "God of the gaps" syndrome, which tries to fit God into things we cannot explain. Even a superficial knowledge of the facts surrounding the origin of life and the new information brought to us through radio astronomy will convince us all that it is unwise to come to trite and simplistic conclusions. However, this is not my intention. Instead, I wish to point out what the implications might be. Since it is widely agreed that the universe had a beginning, we can assume that the universe could not have caused itself. It must have been caused by something or someone who is outside.

Professor P. Davies resists this argument. In a recent book he writes: "When giving lectures on cosmology I am often asked what happened before the big bang. The answer, that there was no 'before,' is regarded with suspicion. But cause and effect are temporal concepts and cannot be applied to a state in which time does not exist; the question is meaningless." But Professor Davies's conclusion is not irresistible, even given the theory that space and time concepts belong to the conditions of this universe. The moment we agree that the universe is finite in duration includes within it the conclusion that something was created from nothing. Professor

Davies has unfortunately fudged the issue in ducking an obvious question. As a scientist he is reluctant to be drawn away from the data before him but, philosophically, the fact that something is created from nothing and continues to be cries out to be answered. This, in essence, is classical Christian teaching; that *ex nihilo* (from nothing) God created. But at this point we have to recognize that that deduction has moved beyond the evidence. That the universe had a beginning in time possibly only proves that it was caused, not that "God" caused it because there is nothing in the data to give us any information regarding the character or the identity of the Causer. Only revelation can give us that information. Nevertheless, it is arguably the case that the existence of an eternal being, the uncreated creator, provides an answer for the question: "Who started it?"

The further reason that the First Cause argument has returned to favor is because thinkers have started to look at the issue not simply from the perspective of cause and effect, but as well from the fact that the universe is a reality and has to be accounted for. Now this is something we are told we should not do. We are told that we cannot move from details in the world to ultimate questions about the universe because there is no identity whatever between the two sets of questions. It's like moving from Aunt Betty's knitting to the Presidency of the United States. But why should not the question of the existence of a divine creator be treated seriously as a proper question? If astronomers and others can speculate seriously about the possibility of thinking beings, similar to ourselves, existing somewhere in the universe, on the basis of no firm evidence, can we not make intelligent deductions about the creation of the universe based more firmly upon our knowledge of our world? A very important book published recently by the Cambridge physicist Dr. Stephen Hawking entitled *A Brief History of Time* argues that the presence of life may point to an act of God although he is at pains to explore alternatives. This theory is called the "Anthropic Principle," which relies upon very precise calculations about the probability that life forms would eventually emerge somewhere in the universe. He writes: "The initial rate of expansion would have to be chosen very precisely for the rate of expansion still to be so close to the critical rate needed to avoid recollapse. This means that the initial state of the universe must have been chosen very carefully indeed if the hot big bang model was correct right back to the beginning of time. It would be very difficult to explain why the universe should have begun in just this way, except as the act of God who intended to create beings like us."

But is it right to make the quantum leap from things within our experience to that without? Why not be content with agnosticism and allow that we shall never know the answer to questions that lurk beyond our world of space and time? I want to argue that it is quite proper for us to ask these questions even though we are prepared to come up against the limits of our knowledge. This, we suggest, is far better than succumbing to the robbery of a culture that has already closed its mind. The question, then, "why does this universe exist at all?" is a proper question because it arises from our perception that things do not generally just happen. There are reasons that things occur, and the possibility that the universe was caused by something or someone who stands in a personal relationship with all created things is not something we can just dismiss. That the present state of play in astronomical research is leading to the exploration of cosmological theories encourages us to believe that our quest is far from ill-conceived or stupid.

We therefore conclude this section by stating that the "God" hypothesis is not as wild and as improbable as some have claimed. The existence of all that is fairly cries out for an explanation, and the striking intelligibility of creation suggests the probability of an intelligent mind behind all the things that are. The Princeton physicist Professor Freeman Dyson stated in a BBC broadcast: "I do feel like an alien in the universe. The more I study the details of its architecture the more evidence I find that the universe in some sense must have known that we were coming."

4

A Personal Creator?

IN THE LAST CHAPTER WE WERE THINKING ABOUT THE SIGNS OF rationality in the world that give rise to the conviction that God exists. We saw that there is in humanity a somewhat innate feeling or possibly even an assumption that "someone" is behind all this. Our agnostic friends sometimes tell us that they have difficulty believing in God but we remind them that not believing in God may possibly be a more problematic undertaking. When experts can show us with models of electrons and neutrons how it was possible for the big bang to occur spontaneously out of nothing, we find ourselves asking, "But how, philosophically, can anything occur out of nothing? In light of the fact that we are inescapably part and parcel of the world and universe, is it not possible that the conscious and intelligent life we possess is not simply an extraordinary accident but actually reflects the nature of creation?"

For those who are young at heart Walt Disney's wonderful film *Love Bug* is an enjoyable feast of escapism. It is the story of a Volkswagen car that is discovered to have a strange personal identity. Odd things happen when people drive it; it takes off by itself and appears to know what people are saying about it even though it cannot communicate directly with them. Its devoted mechanic bursts out at one point: "It isn't just a bundle of parts, sprockets, pistons, and gears—it's Herbie!" Of course nobody seriously watches films like that believing that a mechanical thing can think, make logical decisions, and have emotions, but as I watched it again quite recently I found myself wondering what we mean by such words as "person," "personality," "mind," and, especially, "consciousness." To be a person, we are all agreed, is to have a conscious will and to be able to form rational opinions and make decisions. This is what Herbie was supposed to have and this idea—so improbably—gave to the film its hilarious character.

The question of consciousness raises the issue of the boundary between mind and matter as well as the fundamental disagreement between the believer in God and the materialist. The materialistic position assumes that everything in creation is reducible to material elements; there is nothing that cannot be explained in scientific terms. We must leave to one side many of the elements in this long-standing argument and concentrate instead on the problem of what we mean by consciousness. The more we consider it, the more mysterious it appears to be. Let us consider, for example, our experience of thought. On the one hand, I can have thoughts that are obviously connected to human needs and desires. "How I am looking forward to that steak tonight!" we might find ourselves thinking. Such reactions lend support to the materialist argument of the connection between the physical and mental. But at other times, as I write, and as you read, our minds are full of abstract ideas that appear to have little connection with material things. We find our minds soaring above physical desires and reaching toward a realm of "being" where we feel naturally at home. For this reason, it has long been the opinion of thinkers down the centuries that the existence of "mind" is an obvious proof of God. John Locke, the English philosopher, wrote: "If then there must be something eternal, let us see what sort of being it must be. It is very obvious to reason that it must necessarily be a cogitative being. For it is as impossible to conceive that bare incogitative matter should produce a thinking intelligent being, as that nothing should of itself produce matter."

There are strengths and weaknesses with Locke's argument. The weaknesses are twofold; philosophical and physical. The philosophical problems start with Locke's assumption that the incogitative matter cannot produce intelligence. That may be the case, a philosopher friend will tell us, but it does not follow logically. It might possibly be the case that inanimate things may reach a state of development when consciousness begins. The evolutionary record shows that highly-developed species have emerged from more

primitive forms of life—at the very least we must acknowledge that possibility. The physical problem with Locke's
assertion is that we know for a fact that there is a direct link
between brain events and mental events. A blow on the head
may lead to the loss of consciousness or memory, or something more serious may result. Damage to the physical brain
can have an effect on speech and, even more terribly, lead to
mental derangement and loss of personal identity. We all
know of people who through senile dementia have dete-
riorated tragically. The clear evidence is that there is a link
between the brain and consciousness whether this is causal
or not.

It would seem then that Locke's argument is fatally dam-
aged by the way the physical brain is affected by material
events and by the way it in turn affects what we call the mind.
But this would be a superficial judgment because the case
that they are identical has not been proved. Indeed, this is
where Locke's argument is strong and where extreme materialism is very weak. For the materialist, consciousness is the
accidental epiphenomenon of the brain's activity. That is to
say, thought at every level is an immediate result of brain
states. Some have concluded that as the terms are virtually
synonymous they talk of the "mind-brain." But the invention
of an unattractive new word does not solve an old problem.
Is it in fact the case that we have to yield the ground to the
materialist and confess that there is no reality to the mind—it
is but the word we give to neural activity in our brains?

Now, we have already accepted that a neural connection
exists between brain and mind. I am not suggesting that when

I think of a brilliant idea and cry "Eureka" that this has been done independently of my brain by a ghost-like "mind" that lives somewhere within me. Of course not. The complex computer that we call the human brain is obviously being pulled into service when we argue, think, contemplate, and decide. But it is being pulled into service and not doing it all by itself! Roger Sperry, the neuro-psychologist who discovered the differential functions of the brain's cerebral hemispheres, has directly contradicted the reductionists who argue that the consciousness is nothing more than the outcome of the psychological events in the body. He points to the extreme unlikelihood of non-mental functions creating mental activities (and thus, independently, supports Locke's argument mentioned earlier) and he argues for a directive principle in us that is rational and conscious. He states that "mind is that which moves matter in the brain." That is to say, without denying the mind-body relationship, he rejects a materialistic basis for conscious thought as an inadequate explanation of the complex brain-mind relationship. Human choosing, of course, lends us many useful illustrations of the way the purely physical side of life may be dominated by higher principles. Let us look at one illustration. We all know the tremendously strong pull in us all to survive. It is natural to shrink from pain, violence, and extreme danger. But how often we hear stories of people who have done heroic acts in the face of this natural instinct for survival as, for example, when a person flings himself in front of a terrorist in order to save another human being. Such overtly "irrational" behavior (in the sense that it is not in our own interest to do this) can only be explained by altruistic motives shaped by ideas of love, justice, and God, which are beyond the reach of the purely physical. Somehow, there is something profoundly human in such choosing that cannot be classified under a materialistic category. Our mental experience of abstract and pure thought mocks a simplistic identification between such happenings and neurological states. We all are aware of ourselves as persons who, while having physical emotions, bodily experiences, sensations, and mental events, cannot be limited to just one set of them. Our consciousness of life and the way cerebral thought has shaped the world places us over and against nature in some ways, as well as within it.

What then do we make of the connection between the brain and the conscious mind? Are we faced with a dualism of mind and body? This cannot be, and for some of the reasons given above would be unacceptable. When we think of the powerful mind of Einstein, or the brilliance of Shakespeare, or the intuition, commitment, and scholarship of Madame Curie, we find ourselves rejecting the notion that all such activity is nothing more than an intricate network of nerve endings and pulsating electrical currents. No doubt such elements are included in the process but it is surely not enough to convey the reality of mind in our experience and life in general. No—what we might postulate is the strong possibility of a directive conscious intelligence, which is given to us as human beings and separates us from the rest of the animal kingdom.

With whom then do we share this quality or faculty? The answer we have the temerity to suggest is that this quality of conscious life is not a freak event that just happened to occur to a certain species but, rather, is something that links us with the heart of the universe. This consciousness is also personal, which of course Herbie could never be!

But it is proper to ask a further question at this point. "Do we really have evidence that there is a directive and intelligent principle in the universe?" It hardly seems so when we take into account some of the problems we glanced at in Chapter Two. However, when we talk about intelligence, two things spring immediately to mind: purpose and design. When a fashion designer is creating his or her Autumn Collection, these two principles are obviously central. The purpose may have beauty and elegance as the primary objectives, with warmth probably as a very poor third. The "creator" purposes to arrive at an article that expresses his image of gracefulness. Indeed, the word *creation,* so frequently used by fashion designers, reveals the intention to innovate in a wholly revolutionary way. The design, we might say, is the outworking of the scheme, as a beautiful gown is created and eventually modelled. That intelligence is at work in dress design is sometimes questioned mischievously by some of us, but no doubt to those who are the purchasers, it is all self-evident. They are convinced that a brilliant and creative mind has caught hold of their needs.

When this kind of argument is translated into the quest to find purpose and intelligence in creation generally, it is sometimes called the *teleological argument* after the Greek word *telos* meaning "goal" or "end." So, we have to ask: "Are there clear evidences in life that a conscious, intelligent Principle designed this puzzling universe?" The evidence cannot be said to be conclusive. On the one hand there appear to be clear signs of purpose. No one can deny them. We find it in nature as well as in human life. In nature life works uniformly to plans encoded in the genetic code of a plant or animal. Things grow according to their kind. There is a wonderful beauty and symmetry about the order of creation. As we saw in the last chapter, the scientist working in his laboratory cannot do his work without this as a basic datum of research. This givenness of purpose gives life its meaning and has led to humanity attaining the level of civilization that we now enjoy.

But, we have to say again, who can deny the existence of those elements that appear to refute the idea that there is a personal intelligence behind all living things? Take the apparent randomness of creative life. It hardly seems possible that a benign creator is behind the tortuous fortunes and misfortunes of evolution in which savagery, disease, and wantonness seem to be the shape of things. When we consider the undoubted order of life, we pause when we meet the terrible order of cancer division or the volcanic disaster that destroys the lives of thousands. "God be praised!" say the devout parents of a teen-ager rescued from that volcanic eruption. "God's will be done" pray the bereaved parents of another teen-ager killed in the same disaster. But where is God in it all? Surely, says the skeptic, the evidence all around us compels us to believe that there is no such thing as a personal intelligence behind all things. Our experience of such terrible acts seems to contradict the hypothesis of a loving creator. So, some people conclude, all we need say is that life needs order for there to be life and this creates the illusion that a rational being stands behind it all.

This point does seem very plausible until one considers that order outweighs disorder in the scheme of things. Indeed, the history of creation reveals the outworking of purpose (even if, for the moment, we desist in surmising whether that is personal or blind) as the movement from the primitive to more advanced forms of life proceeds steadily onwards. Of course there are facts in creation that seem to contradict the notion of an intelligent purpose behind the universe, but in noting these at this point we should not minimize the existence of the good, the glorious, and the beautiful that dominate the created order.

When we consider the fact of *design* the same ambivalent picture appears and it is not my intention to *prove* the existence of God from such evidences of design that I may be able to extract from creation. It may be recalled that Archdeacon Paley attempted to prove the existence of God from design. He was convinced that the world showed clear signs of purposeful creation and argued that nature's design greatly surpasses human ingenuity in art, science, and human thought. He argued that if one found a watch on a moor, one would not assume that the watch came there by chance but one would reasonably deduce that a watchmaker existed somewhere. So, he said, the universe is very much like a watch. We find many things in it that seem to be made up of parts that work together to achieve a certain goal. Just as we reason the existence of a watchmaker from the watch, so we might fairly assume the existence of a personal Deity from the existence of the universe.

There is a rather fatal flaw in Paley's argument—which is simply that the relationship between a watch found on a moor and the universe is hardly an identical one. The observer is outside the first but inside the second. I mean by this, that when I argue from watches to other events in the natural world I am the observer of an article that I know has been fashioned by human intelligence. In the case of the universe my position as an observer is different. I am more like a goldfish in a bowl, speculating if anything exists outside my bowl—even if there is a bowl! This weakens greatly the force of the argument. It is clear then that the starting point is going to be very different.

A second problem is that it seems that Paley has smuggled into his argument categories that are questionable. As I pointed out above, the person who finds the watch has already encountered watches before and that is why he is able to say that it has been designed by a person. So J.S. Mill commented, "If I found a watch on a moor I should infer that it had been left by a human being. The inference would not be for design but because I know that watches are made by men." So it looks as though Paley has innocently introduced confusion by supposing that there is some correlation between a watch and the world around. The first is known to us because it is created by human workmanship; the other dwarfs us by its immensity and mystery.

Indeed, Paley's argument seemed to meet its doom once and for all when Darwin's theory of Natural Selection appeared, which seemed to argue so persuasively that design is brought about not by a personal Intelligence behind all things but by natural factors that favored the development of certain species, which arose by chance.

But Paley's argument does in fact present some useful points. It has recently come back into favor and we must consider the reason why. For a start, it is now well known that Darwin's theory of Natural Selection is not exactly what he claimed for it. It is not as chanceless and as random as he supposed. Running through the stream of evolution is a family likeness that links parents to offspring in each generation. It is sometimes said of a new baby that he is a "chip off the old block" or "how like his mother." We expect to find differences that enshrine originality, of course, but it is usually set in the continuity between parent and child. This steady identity is as important for the continuation of the species as are the variations that introduce the new. It is possible then to hold that the general shape of Paley's theory may still be maintained because it is concerned about the purposiveness that suggests the activity of a personal God. As F. R. Tennant so trenchantly put it: "the survival of the fittest presupposes the arrival of the fit." We can accept, then, Paley's basic argument that the world provides many examples of happenings geared to goals and to certain ends. Eyes function in order for people to see—and not the other way round.

Professor C.A. Coulson used to say that very few scientists can avoid the language of teleology because of the principle of order latent in the very nature of things. In fact it is difficult to refute Paley's premise that our overwhelming experience of life is of myriad happenings that are shaped to certain ends.

Paley's argument may, indeed, be found more attractive if we take his general principle of intelligibility rather than concentrating upon his analogy of the correlation between a watch and the world. J.S. Mill was quite right to observe that the problem with the watch illustration is that its plausibility rests on the fact that we have *already* encountered watches. Nevertheless, we defend Paley by saying that his contention was that if we have never come across a watch before it would be the principle of design that would impress us. Paley's interest, of course, was not in watches but on a much deeper question: "Does the universe have that quality of design about it?" To which he gave the unequivocal answer, "Yes, in a million different ways—so much so that it dwarfs human ingenuity."

But we are still left with a quandary in spite of Paley's argument. While there is that about the universe that conveys strong suggestions of an intelligent shaping of its parts, we are left with this question: "Is the quality of purpose best explained by the origins of the universe lying in complete chance, however purposive it might now seem to us to be, or really, is it all the product of an Intelligent Source who continues to keep it functioning according to his/its will?"

We shall look at the matter of chance later, but for the time being we simply note that there are those who believe that purpose and design are nothing but the outworking of the world. "Of course the world seems orderly, rational, and intelligible. But this is simply because in order to exist at all it must have these characteristics. A personal God does not come into it whatever. Who knows what random, freak chances led to the creation of all things?" This argument reminds me of the saying: "A hen is an egg's way of producing an egg."

This conclusion, however, has received some trenchant criticisms from an unusual source. Fred Hoyle has for many years been no friend to theists and Christian believers. He has always expressed a hearty contempt for views that argue for a divine origin for the universe. However, in his book *The Intelligent Universe* he presents a view of the created order that comes very close to that being argued in this book. "Did life start by random processes?" he asks. He answers, "Imagine a blindfolded person trying to solve the Rubik cube. The chance against achieving perfect color matching is about 50,000,000,000,000,000,000 to 1. These odds are roughly the same as those against just one of our body's 200,000 proteins having evolved randomly by chance." He argues strongly and cogently against those who assert that life was created spontaneously and therefore accidentally in some primordial soup and he suggests the controversial theory that because life could not have come from blind chance it must have come to earth from "beings" beyond this planet. Whatever we might think about Hoyle's explanation of intelligent life, central to his point is the conviction that there are strong grounds for believing that the universe is intelligent and information-rich and that it is no accident that humanity has an intelligence that is consonant with that of the universe, which is our home.

I find myself concluding that the inescapable intimacy that binds mankind and nature together leads to the conclusion that "mind," instead of being an accidental intruder into the realm of matter, is intrinsic to life. The universe, said Sir James Jeans in a celebrated speech, "begins to look more like a great thought than like a great machine." If that is the case, as I believe it to be, we are given an insight into the nature of the creator who has poured his intelligence as well as his life into the remarkable cosmos that is our home.

So back to Herbie. What would we have made of it if Herbie really were an intelligent, thinking thing? Very likely we would consider this "thing" a person, however unusual its appearance or however outside our experience this phenomenon was. Because only "persons" can understand, think, or reason and it is only with persons that we can enter into relationships of the deepest kind. At a much deeper level of personhood we judge a person by his or her moral behavior and capacity to love, honor, and respect others. It is in these qualities that Christians find the full flowering of their idea of what it is to be a person. That God is a person they have no doubt, because he has shown himself to be that in Jesus Christ.

5

Does Life Have Any Meaning?

For most of us life conveys a real sense of meaning that we find in the rhythm and joys of life. The majority of our contemporaries live life with a sense of hope although, we have to acknowledge, for most people it is the immediate that concerns them—this year's holiday, family celebrations, or getting a worthwhile job with a decent salary. To lose hope, to lose the sense of worth or meaning, is to lose everything. So then, most of us project a great deal of meaning into our daily lives. All the precious values of human existence keep us going. Without them we could not, and probably would not want to, carry on. That is why we sometimes hear of elderly couples who, when one dies, the partner finds himself or herself totally unable to live in any meaningful way again.

All real meaning has been taken away from life itself and death together is the only way out. But, equally, that is why many of us take such pleasure and expend so much anxiety on our loved ones because they are for us the meaning of life. We cannot contemplate life without them.

But meaning and value in ordinary life we can accept and understand. Such experiences and relationships make our existence valuable. But is there value and meaning in the universe itself? Can it be that it has been created by a Maker who loves us eternally and who pours meaning into this mysterious creation?

From some points of view the answer might seem to be "no" and the irresistible conclusion is that there is no ultimate or cosmic meaning. We can all think of events that do not fit in with our understanding of a loving God. Take those stories in our newspapers that tell of young children dying of cancer, of accidents that leave children orphans, of tragedies that simply numb us. There does not seem to be any rationale or structure to life, which leads ineluctably to the conclusion that we live in a meaningful universe. Of course, this kind of problem is not new. We must not fall into the hubris of thinking that only modern people think such thoughts. The book of Job in the Old Testament is all about this. It appeared that Job found it easy to believe and trust in God when things were going well. Problems began for his belief when everything—including his health—was taken away. We are not now going to take up the issue of pain and evil because that will be considered in the next chapter. The issue that concerns us now is the implication of this: whether there are real grounds for saying that there is meaning and value in life that transcend us and our individual value systems. Again, we must express our concern that our culture has very success-fully communicated a moral blight over our society and robbed us of the sense of the transcendent. The separation of "right" and "wrong" from the content of the Christian faith means that morality has lost its ideological basis and few perceive it. The result is that morality has been separated from ideas of God and has been privatized; it has been made largely a matter of personal choice. The corollary of this is serious because if there is no divine basis behind human values, all forms of ethical theory are subjective and have as much permanence as sandcastles. So it is important to con-sider whether there are ultimate values in this universe to which we are bound in a permanent relationship of being.

The Christian faith declares firmly that there are, but for the sake of objectivity we must remind ourselves that these cannot be proved in the way that I can prove a mathematical theorem. All we are able to point to are clues that there are values that point beyond us to Someone for whom our behavior and value systems are important. Nevertheless, I am confident in saying that these are real clues that arch toward the possibility that morality is not a luxury that comes with advanced civilizations—which is somehow dispensable, if we feel inclined—but is anchored in the being and rhythm of the world and, as a result, is inseparable from humankind's nature to respond to a morality that stands over and against us.

The first and most significant clue is that of morality itself. Moral standards are familiar to us all. Most of us have been shaped by valued systems from our childhood. Those of us in the West have been influenced by a Judaeo-Christian morality that embraces both the Ten Commandments and the teaching of Jesus. In other parts of the world other moral codes have given to people a sense of purpose and worth. What is common to all developed moral codes is the assumption that we are moral and spiritual beings who must respond to claims that transcend those codes. That is to say, the moral codes together invite us all to grow into a dignity and humanity that is our destiny. But sometimes we wonder whether it is the case that moral codes themselves are nothing more than value systems thrust on people by circumstances, by the conquerors, and by convention.

Let us consider the issue more carefully. There have been various attempts to explain the moral element in human nature. Some have held that the real motive in conduct is self-interest. We do the things that promote our welfare or happiness, whether it be as individuals or societies. The classic expression of this, ironically enough, comes from the book of Job where Satan, in his discussion with God about the goodness of Job, says with a sneer: "Does Job serve God for nought?" The implication of the question is that if all Job's possessions were taken away, the root of his goodness would soon wither away. According to this view then, once people find that goodness is no longer a paying proposition, they will give it up. But the whole thrust of the book of Job is that integrity of life is more important than one's life. "Though he slay me, yet will I trust him," says Job of his God. And what Job wrestles with you and I know as well—that while there may be some whose morality stems from avarice, the only self-interest that the majority of us recognize in ethical decisions is the interest of our better self when we know that a certain course will help others and we say that it is "right."

Another, and even more popular, theory is that all morality is nothing more than society's control of its members. According to this idea our ideals have their source in the discovery that certain ways of living and certain virtues promote the welfare of the tribe, and from these patterns of life, society has evolved its norms in order to safeguard its life and protect the unity of the family. So, because the habit of theft was bad for the community, the community forbade it and honesty became an obligatory moral principle. Because killing one another destroys the harmony and unity of the community, murder is forbidden. So this theory enthrones the community as the real author of moral values. This looks like a very plausible theory and is commonly accepted by many today. Its attraction may reside in the evidence that certain values have clearly been shaped by the needs of the community and changing needs have modified or even rejected what once was thought to be unalterable. Take, for example, the place of women in society. It wasn't all that long ago when Western society considered it wrong for women to have the vote or even a profession. Their place was in the home—that was where God had placed them and they should be content with their lot. Few would argue that these days. So it seems that society plays a most significant part in forming our moral codes.

But there are two questions that reveal the weakness of this argument. First, why should it be better for us, in the long run, to be brave rather than cowardly, honest rather than dishonest, pure rather than impure, faithful rather than unfaithful? For such qualities do not always coincide with the benefit of the community. It may well be to the advantage of a tribe to extend its boundaries by pillaging, rape, and widespread destruction. It may seem, then, that such actions are acceptable because they advance the good of the tribe. I have not met anybody who would argue this. In fact, such qualities of honesty, goodness, and bravery—to name but a few—do work out for the well-being of the community in spite of the experience that they do not always work out for the material benefit of those who live such generous lives. At the international level we are discovering today that goodwill, humanity, freedom, forgiveness, and tolerance are among the values that advance civilization and that national selfishness and moral anarchy are threatening the very being of human existence. There can be only one explanation for the existence of such "soft" altruistic standards, and that is that life is meant to be lived in this way—that such laws of conduct are not imposed on us through the needs of the community but rather they emerge from the constitution of our being.

The second question is this: Is it not the case that moral codes have arisen from charismatic leaders and from minority groups, rather than from society as a whole? It is an undeniable fact that in nearly every case when a great moral teacher has appeared, society has at first rejected him because his message has condemned the practices and values of society. We note, for example, that so many pioneers of reform have had to go to the stake for their beliefs or have had to struggle for recognition. If society originated the moral laws, why was it that when the prophets of the Old Testament and the greatest of all moral teachers, Jesus Christ, appeared, society rejected their teachings, and authority?

It seems very clear then that the sense of moral obligation has deeper roots than our own social advantage. It is not in fact the case that our own good is the reason that "goodness" has authority over us. Rather, we seek the good because it is right and not because it is to our advantage. It is only when we are prepared to listen to the voice of conscience and follow it that our true humanity and calling are discovered. Andre Gide—an immoral libertine with a nagging conscience—spoke more perceptively than he realized when he wrote: "Je ne suis qu'un petit garçon qui s'amuse, double de pasteur protestant qui l'ennuie" (I am just a little boy having fun, with a Protestant minister nagging away inside me). That is to say, he was aware, however dimly, of obligations that challenged his instincts and desires.

So the conditional and relativizing attitude that dismisses all morality as stemming from the needs of society must be rejected as inadequate. Most of us do not view ethical responses in that way anyway. We regard morality as having an overarching and eternal significance. Morality is true regardless of time and place. Murder, we assume, would always be wrong whether one is a Caligula living in the first century or Hitler living in the twentieth century. Standards of goodness, decency, honor, integrity, or honesty (among other virtues that make a civilization great) are true whatever the time and place. We do, therefore, find ourselves postulating "absolute" standards of right and wrong. This was at the heart of the famous debate between Bertrand Russell and the Roman Catholic philosopher, Thomas Coplestone. Russell had declared that there were no absolute values as such; all we could say was that there exist values that we deem important. To this, Coplestone cited the then recent Nuremburg trials in which Nazi criminals had been convicted of crimes against humanity. If there are no absolutes, he said, it was not immediately obvious what the conceptual basis for the trials was. Crimes against humanity suggest that there exists a moral standard that all agree the Nazis contravened. Many of those accused could cite that they were carrying out the edicts of the State or following the orders of superiors. Yet the Trial expressed the unanimous verdict of the nations that those condemned had broken a moral law that was absolute and eternal. There can be little doubt that Coplestone had the better of that argument because when we are faced with issues of such magnitude, we are convinced of the reality of moral facts that call us to a higher standard of humanity than that of our present experience.

It is true that we do not need the hypothesis God for such a morality. I want to make it very clear that even in a godless universe most of us would still expect cruelty to be wrong and evil. We all know people who do not have a "faith" to speak of but who live honorable and good lives. Nevertheless in a godless universe the concepts of "wrongdoing" and "goodness" are going to have completely different meanings from that of a morality anchored in belief in God. For example, I may say as a non-believer: "Although I do not believe in God I still firmly believe that it is right to be a person of integrity. For me moral standards are vital for society, my personal life, and the community that I belong to." It is obvious, however, that the basis of my ethics will depend for its validity not upon a God who gives to such values eternal significance, but upon our built-in feelings that certain things are wrong and others are right.

Secondly, while it would be the honorable thing to be good and righteous in a godless universe, it does not seem to be the most logical way of performing. If this life is all, then choosing an ethic that means putting other people first seems an astonishingly illogical way to live. As Professor Oliver O'Donovan puts it: "No earthly good can be worth dying for unless there is heavenly good that is worth living for." This observation goes to the heart of the malaise of Western civilization. The loss of the transcendent in our society has led to the questioning of "ultimate sacrifice." Whereas our forebears could face death with equanimity and consider it worthwhile to lay down one's life for another because of the greater hope and destiny to which one was called, this consoling synthesis is no longer at the center of our concept of life. In a world where values are relative and transitory, too great a demand is then placed upon other arguments to make them truly convincing. An example of this is the Falklands

War, which led to the loss of hundreds of lives on both sides. What was the war about? The question of the sovereignty of a small island? A matter of honor? We could well question whether either or both of these things are worth the death of one young soldier, let alone thousands. We might well wonder about the reaction of bereaved wives and families to that war. It is doubtful that they see it as a necessary conflict that justified the deaths of those who went to war. If many years later a deal is struck in which sovereignty passes to the Argentine by gradual stages, would not that very act negate the eternal sacrifices made? The point I am making is the very futility of acts of that nature *if* the values we are living by and dying for are not in some sense eternal and relate to God who gives to life its rationality and meaning. Otherwise such acts are basically tragic and meaningless.

This last conclusion, of course, has been reached by serious philosophers in recent years. Friedrich Nietzsche argued that in the absence of God everything is permitted. This view has been taken up by existential writers like Jean-Paul Sartre for whom the absence of God was not only a terrifying nightmare but also, curiously, a liberating experience because now man has only himself to rely upon and this, Sartre thought, would lead to humanity's growth. But "good" without God makes moral values relative and subordinate to what is "good" for us. It will be seen that this line of argument may lead into a sharp individualism (what is good for "me") and it may equally have a nihilistic edge to it (if we are all doomed to annihilation and meaning does not exist, why bother?).

I have already agreed, however, that even if God did not exist there would be reason to be moral beings. I am not advocating that if this universe is a random happening we should all behave like animals. Of course not. We would all affirm that human life, our love for others, and our respect for their views would demand from each one of us a morality that is in accord with the well-ordering of society. The "golden rule" of Jesus—"Do unto others as you would have others do unto you"—applies equally to an atheistic culture as to one founded on Christian insights. But I would like to go on to suggest that although I do not need God in order to be a moral person, at the very least the existence of God gives to morality a depth, coherence, and rational framework that is otherwise lacking. You see, within the Christian tradition we can easily explain why non-religious people are moral people—it is because they too are made in the image of God and bear the stamp of his likeness. It is an element of our theology that to be a human being at all is to be aware of moral strivings, feelings of guilt and sin, and feelings of freedom and slavery. At the heart of this understanding of humanity is the teaching that humanity has gone fundamentally astray, that we are unable to find the true God unaided because we are fallen and sinful. This is the famous doctrine of *original sin* which, simply stated, means that there is a fundamental flaw in our human nature that stops us from becoming the kind of people we would like to be. G.K. Chesterton once said perceptively that of all Christian doctrines original sin was the only directly provable one because the evidence was all too obvious.

But why should "God" give to morality a more rational framework than, say, the argument that morality is but the outworking of conventions in society, or our corporate experience that certain behavior is more satisfactory for us all? I have already answered this to some extent in my observations that for the Christian, God is himself the justification for the way we behave. If I decide, in a country violently opposed to the Christian faith, that I must act in such a way that I could incur the wrath of the State and face the death penalty, I do so because I have a system of transcendental values that is true whatever may happen to me. In a similar way, martyrs for just causes are clearly protesting for values that are not transitory and relative but for things that concern them so deeply that they can only act in that way. So, for example, the political and religious dissidents in Soviet Russia willingly endure separation, physical pain, mockery, and, in some cases, death because they reject as basically inhuman (and godless) a system that allows no other point of view but its own. However, I think we can say a little more than that. It is accepted by many of us that the reality of morality is written in large letters in the actual experience and history of humankind. And it is an agreed assumption, I find, that there are moral facts, absolute areas of "right" and "wrong," which stand over us judging us by standards we all recognize and calling us to a personhood that, as yet, eludes most of us. And I find a tacit acknowledgment by most people that such laws are valid for all people and all time.

We are not, of course, talking about values that may depend upon cultural ways of behavior; matters concerning the smooth running of society and aspects of convention. Rather, our concern is the moral worth that transcends culture. For example, we take it for granted that killing another person in cold blood will be as wrong in A.D. 2500 as it is now. And, for that matter, we cannot conceive of a society in which stealing, lying, cruelty, etc. could ever be considered socially acceptable acts. Not only would they undermine society and eventually destroy it, but we actually do believe that they are wrong, per se. But the heart of the problem is this. While most of us actually *believe* that such acts are wrong, no convincing argument can be adduced to *prove* this fact. Morality cannot prove God, but what it can do is point to him and the values that are at his heart. Such values will be the dignity of humanity, our intrinsic worth, our moral nature, and our ability to respond to claims of "oughtness" and "rightness," our ability to grow in selfless action and love for others, and our capacity for self-sacrifice which, on the face of it, seems madness. All this, and much more, points beyond ourselves and cries for explanation. Does all this simply come from ourselves, or are these elements of a bonding with the divine, which has all the dimensions of an Imperative that cannot be denied or ignored?

Another area that must be examined briefly are those qualities of human existence—art, beauty, and pleasure— that also point beyond ourselves to the possibility of another origin. Just before Christmas in 1986 my wife and I enjoyed a brief holiday near Hereford, England. As I had never visited the Cathedral there before, I decided to spend Saturday afternoon in it. I pushed open the Cathedral doors and was hit by an explosion of sound that filled the place and my soul as well. What I discovered was that in the Cathedral a visiting orchestra and local choir were rehearsing Dvorak's *Te Deum* for an evening concert. The richness of the sound and the beauty of the music were so bewitchingly wonderful that all the listeners on that gray afternoon were taken up into a world very different from the one we were inhabiting. This experience brought home to me the way that music and poetry stand out as marvelous vehicles for the language of the soul. And yet, they need not be seen in that way. The instruments, after all, are only things made by people and the performers are obviously only mortal. Even the music, when reduced to squiggles on paper, does not appear to be any more than the cold symbols of human beings trying to entertain. But that reductionism is dismissed immediately by most of us because we know how music and art in their varying forms can enlarge the human spirit and take us to levels of perception and emotional heights that nothing else can do. Little wonder that such areas of life have been harnessed by religion over the centuries and encouraged by mainstream faiths because of the very evocative force they release.

If this is so, two very important corollaries follow. The first is a challenge to language in our culture. Perhaps the barrenness of spirit today is related to the debasing of language as a mere counter of knowledge. But the world of imagination forces us to ask: Are we not depriving ourselves of a world of color and richness by making the plain meaning primary and the metaphor and poetry of language secondary? Could it not be true that the creative realm—such as literature and art in their many forms—is not external to knowledge and the meaning of life, but an essential component within it, possessing power to comprehend spiritual realities in life? The writer and poet Coleridge was intensely aware of the link between art and faith, between knowledge and religion. He remarked: "When I worship let me unify . . . to be wise I must." Or as the theologian Schleiermacher once observed, "What the word makes clear, music must make alive."

The second observation takes us to the heart of another dichotomy in modern life, namely our tendency to separate faith and life. For the Christian the two are inseparably connected. To be a Christian and to be a human being are essentially one. But for the nonbeliever, Christianity and indeed all faiths are cultural by-products of civilizations, invented to meet human needs and aspirations. They, together with art and any form of knowledge, are aspects of the flowering of human development but have no intrinsic value over and above that.

Yet, the evidence in fact points in the opposite direction. Faith in God is not a cultural accretion but an essential part of culture. Toynbee said long ago: "The great civilizations of the world do not produce the great religions as a kind of cultural by-product; in a real sense the great religions are the foundations on which the great civilizations rest." As far as Christianity is concerned, for more than a millennium it has supplied the meaning and aim of individual and corporate existences. It has fed the living stream of Western culture in such a rich way that our civilization is incomprehensible without it. Yet for the last hundred and fifty years this heritage of faith has been deliberately jettisoned in order to show that science alone—or some other pathway—can provide humanity with a better framework for life. Culture devoid of the faith that gave it birth is but a new name for a new paganism. Chip away at the cement of faith and the foundations of humanity will be seen to be very unstable indeed; strip away firm belief in God and eventually we will start disbelieving in ourselves and everything we hold dear. Well did T.S. Eliot write: "Man is man because he can realise spiritual realities, not because he can invent them."

6

Good, Evil, and God

TWO YEARS AGO MY MOTHER DIED. SHE WAS 76 YEARS OF AGE and she had lived a full and happy life. But her last year had been an absolute hell. Cancer of the tongue had developed, which required radiotherapy. In spite of modern drugs she was in constant pain, and with distress and sadness, we her children watched her losing battle against the disease. Toward the end she went downhill rapidly. I happened to be with her holding her hand when she died. As I looked at her face, wasted away with pain and hardly recognizable as my dear mother, I wondered where God was in this situation. I found myself asking bitterly: "God—here is a Christian lady who has served you faithfully down the years. Now look at the pain and discomfort she has to bear. Is this how you treat your friends?" Of course, I acknowledge that it was grief speaking at that moment. My mother would have been the first to remind me firmly that God's love transcends all evil and all human suffering. Nevertheless, in reacting as I did, I was echoing the experience of millions of people who feel, during times of pain and suffering, the absence of God.

Very few of us doubt that the problem of evil is the single greatest obstacle to faith. The case for God would be simply overwhelming if this issue did not separate intelligent people from the concept of a loving God. We respect those for whom evil forbids faith. However, sadly, yet increasingly, I find people today accepting an attitude that says tacitly there is no personal God behind the things that are, but rather blind, unreasoning fate. "We can't understand it" goes the attitude "but whatever will be, will be." Such a stance is not founded upon careful thought and study but drawn from a culture that has already come to the conclusion that life is purposeless. We have in this matter another example of the way modern people are being conned into adopting an attitude that is simply borrowed from the prevailing, hostile spiritual environment of our time. We need to ask then: Is it a fact that the problem of evil is so overwhelming that it cancels out all arguments for God's presence in the world? We must look at the issues involved.

The problem of evil can be put into two categories. First there is the moral evil caused by man's evil to man. We can think of happenings that create further evil, such as war leading to famine or concentration camps resulting in the suffering of innocent children. In this category we could put the simply awful suffering of the Jewish people in World War II. The estimate of eight million human beings dying, many in the most appalling and degrading ways, will always be an indictment on twentieth-century civilization. At Auschwitz there died completely the concept of man's perfectibility. Until that time there were many people who believed that through self-improvement—education, medical care, etc.— human beings would grow into a god-like state of well-being and grace. There was, it was thought, no limit upon the achievements humankind is capable of. Many believed there was no limit to humankind's destiny. Auschwitz revealed the folly of such grand hopes. But for many committed Jews the nightmare raised the most serious doubts about God's activity with his so-called people. The Jewish writer Milac Makovec explained that his rejection of God stems from the evil in the world: "I cannot combine faith in God with Auschwitz." As mentioned earlier, the Jewish writer, Professor Richard Rubenstein put it more trenchantly: "How can Jews believe in an omnipotent, beneficent God after Auschwitz?" Rubenstein's answer led him to conclude that although there is a "God" of some description we are bereft of him. We stand alone in a cold, silent, unfeeling cosmos, unaided by any purposeful power beyond our own resources. He appeals to his fellow Jews to revise their theology and to reinterpret their faith, which has to find a new form and focus in the preservation of the religious community.

The Jewish experience is not everybody's experience, however. And, we should add, not all Jews are convinced that a radical revisionism is necessary. Yet it crystallizes the central issue as far as person-centered moral evil is concerned. *Why* could God not have intervened? It does not seem beyond God's power—if, that is, he is all-powerful—to intervene in the mess that we make of his creation. We can think of hundreds of examples of the problem and we are left with our questions.

The second category of moral evil is the evil endemic in creation and life. We need only think of little children born with defects that range from a harelip to Down's Syndrome or cancer. We think of tragedies that strike regardless of values of right and wrong. The good are as likely to suffer as the bad in the lottery of life. The case is put in its sharpest form in literature that explores the nature of the world. In Dostoyevsky's *The Brothers Karamazov,* Ivan protests vehemently against a world in which innocent human beings, including children, suffer hideous cruelties at the hands of those who have power over them. Ivan cannot understand how such a world can be the creation of a good God or how a just creator can permit such suffering and fail to use his power on behalf of the victims. The extent of suffering, Ivan believes, points to indifference at the heart of the universe. He is led to renounce Christianity's claims for a good God, courteously refusing a ticket to a heaven that is based on such suffering, by saying, "I renounce the higher harmony altogether. It is not worth the tears of that one tortured child . . ." Yet, we must understand, this passionate expression of atheism comes from an artist who writes from *the side of the Christian faith*. Dostoyevsky does not reject the Christian faith; but he does point at the real world and the real questions that challenge faith.

A similar point is made by Albert Camus in his book *The Plague,* although now from a different point of view. Camus did not share Dostoyevsky's faith but he did share his concern for a world that did not appear to express moral values. Dr. Rieux, one of the central characters in the book, betrays the same angry reaction following the agonizing death of a child. The priest observes that the death is only revolting because we do not understand it and says that: "Perhaps we should love what we cannot understand." The doctor replies angrily, "No, Father! I have a different idea of love. Until my dying day I shall refuse to love a scheme of things in which children are put to torture." We can agree emphatically that Dr. Rieux's response is more "Christian" than that of the priest's, whose superficial attitude seems indifferent and callous. Yet Camus is painfully aware that in rejecting the possibility of God, such concepts as justice, morality, honor, and kindness have to be redefined. "Can one be a saint without God?" asks Tarrou in the same book. The question is never answered even though the book struggles to find the value of human existence in a creation without a creator.

While it is important to feel the awfulness of evil, we must start our discussion of it in the context of good. The fact of the matter is that we do not live in a universe of unmitigated evil. To read some books you would think so. If the cosmos is as blind, irrational, and indifferent as some people claim, truth, beauty, love, meaning, goodness, purity, honesty, and other values become problems themselves and require explanation. It is a fact, as we observed earlier, that for the majority of us life can have great purpose. Evil—seen, that is, from the viewpoint of most of us—is more like an element that breaks into good rather than good interrupting a scheme of things in which evil is the normal currency. The latter is clearly not the case. This planet, for example, is congenial for our well-being and survival. Humankind has flourished and multiplied over the centuries and within our environment there has been a sufficiency of raw products to take us from the cave to the space shuttle. Our supremacy over our habitat may not be enough to prove the necessity of a personal Maker (although Christians believe that this would not be an illogical deduction), but it is consonant with the world as being good, when we take all the elements together.

If that is the case, then, we have to account for the evil in the world and try to explain why God does not intervene when things go wrong. There are at least four possible responses to this issue. We shall leave unconsidered such answers as "evil is only imaginary" or "evil is God's judgment on sinners." The first is clearly and demonstrably wrong and the second, while obviously more plausible as a general truth, does not fit the nature of the evidence because the innocent are involved in suffering. If suffering is the result of personal sin it can't be theirs and, indeed, the theory would make God a monster.

One possible answer is that pain and evil are inevitable consequences of the world being as it is. Swinburne, a modern philosopher, argues that if God wanted to create an environment for humanity's relationship with himself, and its moral and spiritual growth, it has to be a world similar to our own in which wasted suffering and natural evil are present. According to this view, moral and spiritual responses come through the challenges of life. It assumes that in a static universe where there is no conflict, no opposition between good and evil, no disasters and no errors of any kind, humankind would be morally static and moribund.

There is enough truth in this theory to impress. It is agreed that change, trouble, and disorder are elements that spur growth. Certainly our experience of life shows that adversity makes people grow morally and spiritually and draws forth outstanding acts of behavior. There would be no acts of mercy if people were in no danger, no acts of heroism if others did not require saving, no goodness if all were good, and so we could go on. But the argument leaves me unconvinced. I want to ask, how do we know that a perfect world could not produce moral acts such as the ones listed? Why must we assume that a paradise on earth would be morally static? And, for that matter, speaking on behalf of the half-believer or non-believer, we wonder about the long ages of history where natural calamities occurred before humankind's arrival, which had nothing to do with our moral growth. Indeed, this argument suggests that heaven is morally static so that it appears that growth is impossible. Surely this goes against the Christian conviction that life in God has endless, exciting possibilities for growth and development. I for one do not believe in a heaven that is morally stagnant and I am equally sure we don't need battles and adversity to make this possible!

A second theory argues that free will requires a world that is not self-limited in any form. According to this argument, God's ultimate purpose in creating for himself human persons, made for his glory and made in his image, entails the creation of a world in which freedom is at its heart. In such a world, God necessarily limits himself and takes a risk in allowing humankind to have such freedom that human sinfulness is allowed full scope and evil may run riot. Freedom and free will must, according to this argument, be real gifts of God and part of the constituent make-up of life, otherwise we will end up with a crazy world in which God keeps leaping in and out to intervene when his favorites get into trouble. Such a world and a God would be ludicrous. Freedom and free will will result in mistakes, error, and growth. Such a theory is not without its attractions. We know that much evil is directly attributable to man's inherently cruel and sinful tendencies. The holocaust is a sad example of this fact. It cannot be the case, we may think, that God must be blamed for something that has to be laid at humanity's door.

But, again, there are aspects to this that trouble me. Does free will demand a world in which God apparently abandons the world to the devices of evil? If free will comes from God, then it seems like God was unable to make a world in which that freedom does not result in evil. The point must be pressed home; we might well ask, "What is God doing when suffering and evil out of all proportion are afflicted by evil people on the innocent?" And this is at the heart of the matter—we are not talking about suffering in reasonable proportions to the situation but gross, shocking evils that defy description. This is the point that some radical Jewish theologians make about the holocaust. The awfulness of the situation raised the most serious doubts concerning their central understanding of God. Brought up on the belief that he is the faithful god of Israel, his people questioned their age-old faith when they went through agony. So, while it is possible to understand that God restrains his power because he has given free will to his creatures, the *apparent* abnegation of his power resulting in the experience of absence of God and the triumph of evil cries out for an answer. Indeed, do we not find at this point the cry of the cross: "My God, why have you forsaken me?"

A third theory associated with Bernard Lonergan, perhaps the greatest Roman Catholic philosopher of the twentieth century, questions the use of the phrase "problem of evil." What do we mean when we call evil a "problem"? he asks. He points out that we commonly judge God's purposes in the world by whether or not a thing occurs that is good or bad for us. A friend is tragically killed, someone known to us is struck down by a rare disease, a child dies. Because such things happen that do not accord with our understanding of how God ought to act, we conclude that the universe is inexplicable and "evil" is a negation of good. But, argues Lonergan, we cannot assess the matter in such personal terms. Our criterion is irrationality when, in fact, the world is intensely rational. Things occur because there are reasons for them doing so. Earthquakes happen for physical reasons; the avalanche falls because of factors that can be understood scientifically; the disease is attributable to causes that can be

known. So, if one lives in California or in Bangladesh, we
must not complain too bitterly when the earthquake or the
flood occurs—because we know that these places are sus-
ceptible to such physical "evils." We call the problem "evil"
because we judge the order of the world by whether or not
it works to our well-being.

There is an awesome logic about Lonergan's approach and
I happen to think that he is close to the truth of the matter.
But a few problems remain, particularly with regard to the
nature of God. Even if he has removed the element of the
problem of evil, he has created a further one about God
himself. What is Lonergan's God like who allows such things
to happen? What are his purposes in allowing that little child
to die before her time? We can allow the irresistible logic that
demands that leukemia may end in death if unhealed, but it
is happening to a child made, according to Christian faith, in
the image of God and it is God who directly or indirectly is
the cause of the problem.

However, I do find Lonergan's theory helpful and suggest
that its insights should be held in tension with our fourth
theory, which takes up the theme of *purpose*. We know that
one of the reasons we can accept the death of an old man,
while bitterly deploring the death of a young mother, has
something to do with the unfulfilled nature of human destiny.
We can say of the first, "He has had a fine life. Sad to see him
go, though. We shall miss him, but he was failing toward the
end." But of the latter death we are inclined to say, "How very
sad. What a loss to us all. What a happy person she was. And
the children are going to miss her awfully."

Our attitude to both situations is linked with our understanding of fulfillment. "Good" and "evil" are anchored in our estimate of a worthwhile life. What has happened has not lived up to our natural expectations. It is not fair that the young woman should be taken at that time. We rebel against the injustice of it. But what we are failing to observe in drawing these conclusions is that the issue is not merely about evil, but evil in the context of good. We are implicitly granting that the badness occurs in the setting of success—of good being present. We are passionately aware of the presence of justice, good, human dignity, and other values, and there is a diminution of such qualities, we feel, in this or that particular case. So, for example, that sick child is a child who is sick. That is to say, she is a human person who at this point is being held back from her destiny to be a whole and healthy girl. In Christian theology this idea is sometimes called "privation." That is, the person is affected by something that deprives her, either temporarily or permanently, of the possibility of growing to her full potential. Thus, to say that a loaf of bread is "bad" is not to say that it is not a loaf of bread but that it fails to come up to our expectations. Seen, then, from this perspective, the presence of evils in the world are elements that deprive us of what we assume to be our rightful heritage as human beings.

Two observations may be made of this theory immediately. First, it takes seriously the fact of evil, but it does not directly attribute it to God. Evil is the non-obtaining of good. It is the falling short of the perfection that is its true destiny and is an incompleteness that is not God's will.

Second, the Christian faith does not consider evil in any
way final or decisive. However awful it may be, and however
its tragic dimensions may affect every aspect of human life,
evil cannot cut God's people off from their destiny in him. In
other words evil will not have the last word; God's purposes
will triumph over the short-lived evils brought upon human
beings by a world in which the human drama is set. As some
theologians put it, we need to see this world from the viewpoint of *sub specie aeternatis,* from God's ultimate purpose
for his creation; failure to take this into our reckoning will
result in a one-dimensional view of human existence that is
the bankrupt legacy of twentieth-century thought. Let us take,
for example, an analogy from a tadpole pool. Let us allow
that within the pool relationships there is constituted the heart
of morality. Good and evil are seen in terms of their welfare.
So, if a thing happens that makes them happy, wealthy, or
"fulfilled," that is "good." If something happens that seems to
deny their destiny, we call that happening "bad." But, still
playing with our analogy, we allow that the true destiny of
the tadpoles is not to live and die as tadpoles but to grow up
to become frogs. Now, what we tacitly assumed to be "good"
(from within the pond) for the tadpoles is seen not to be so
in this different perspective. Similarly, if this life is all, we
might well judge goodness and its opposite from such criteria
as the length of life, standard of living, peace and prosperity,
the happiness of our children, and so on. But if our destiny
finds its true fulfillment in an eternal fellowship with God,
which is begun in this life and flowers not only in a fulfilled
life now (for many of us) but also into a glorious life beyond

death, then we begin to see that God may have a different understanding of the meaning of human existence and the place of struggle, tragedy, defeat, and weakness in its constitution.

We have glanced at four possible approaches to the problem of evil. We have made no attempt to minimize the revulsion we all feel in the presence of this ugly blasphemy, which distorts not only human life but the whole of creation. Nevertheless we have also seen that when we remove it from its context in goodness, or exaggerate its prominence, we do not do justice to a world that carries the marks of a good creator. Evil is the blackness in the tapestry of life, but there are many other colors there, and, as one of the theories mentioned above observed, we need the blackness in order for the other colors to be seen in all their splendor. That may well be the case. However, I will not pretend that the problem of evil has been solved or that the theist can easily avoid the difficult task of explaining its presence in a world that we claim to be the creation of a loving heavenly Father.

There is a final point that we must observe if we really wish to have a rounded view of the whole matter. The Christian world view does not include a God out there who watches helplessly, yet with compassion, as his people suffer. We believe firmly in wholehearted, committed, suffering love. Christian faith is summed up in the good news that the cross is the gateway of life with God and there we see God identifying with sin and suffering. To leave the cross out is to miss something important about the character of God and the nature of his love.

It may seem that the problem is essentially unresolvable. In one sense we have to admit it is. Reason cannot take us all the way into believing in a God who created the world and gives us its meaning. We acknowledge that we all bring to such a question our own presuppositions and prejudices. I am a Christian, and it is impossible for me to consider the issue from the standpoint of unbelief. I cannot suspend either my critical faculties or my faith. And neither can an agnostic reading these words. He, too, approaches the issue with his own set of prejudices and presuppositions. It may seem then that such fixed positions cancel each other out and we have to be content with a resigned agnosticism. But the Christian will want to answer that faith cannot be built on reason or objective facts alone; it also comes from the experience of Christians who claim that they have met the living God. In Christ they have found him, not as an indifferent, cold deity who leaves them to get on with the task of living, but as a father who cares and loves. To the question of "experience" we must now turn.

7

What Does Experience Say about God?

S O FAR IN THIS BOOK OUR EXPLORATION INTO GOD HAS BEEN limited to rational argument. We have been trying to show that belief in God is "reasonable" and can be accepted by modern Western people. Now I happen to believe that this is the case, and I am not alone in holding this conviction with confidence. For literally millions of people, only acceptance of a God who creates and cares makes sense of this world. But such an acceptance falls far short of the Christian God who confronts men and women not as a mysterious deity but as the "living God," the creator God who is a being to be worshipped and adored. I, personally, cannot work up much enthusiasm for a First Cause or a "merely probable God" who is just the abstraction of human minds. Such a belief would be too dreary for words and would not propel faith in the way that a real encounter with the living God would.

This powerful confrontation has been viewed in many different ways, but all these forms focus on what we call "experience." People claim that they have "found" God, "met" God, felt his "touch" of power, peace, comfort, or challenge, and experienced his "love." This should not be too surprising, of course. If there is a personal God, as Alec Vidler used to say, it is in our personal experience that we should expect to find the strongest evidence of his existence. Indeed, experiences claimed to be of God and of messages from him are so widespread, not only in time but also throughout the world, that they must be examined to see if here there are intimations of the presence of God. The problem, however, is that of evaluating the myriad forms that the experience of God takes and assessing the reality or falsehood of such claims. Are they, we have to ask, proofs of God as such? Certainly they seem to be so for the person who claims to have met God, but what about those of us who stand by skeptically and listen?

Now in the majority of cases we cannot deny the sincerity of those who say that they have met God. But how do we know that it is God who they have met? After all, if my house is burglarized and I catch a glimpse of the burglar fleeing from the house and say to the police, "Jack Brown is the culprit," the reasonable deduction is that I have met Mr. Brown before; otherwise I could not have known his name. So when a person says, "Last week I met God," or "I had a wonderful experience of his love," we could reasonably deduce that

God was already a familiar concept to her, otherwise the claim would not have been put in that form. The suspicion, then, is that some degree of pre-conditioning has gone on to make the idea of God a reality before the experience takes place. It is a fact, for example, that the phenomena of appearances of the Blessed Virgin Mary, which occur almost exclusively in Roman Catholic countries, strongly suggest to the outsider that such visions have been influenced by popular Catholic expectation that when God appears directly to people, he is going to take a Marian shape. I am not for one minute questioning the reality of such experiences, but the facts compel us to note the way in which background of belief shapes the nature of the experience. Of course it is arguably the case, we must admit, that no one can come to an experience without some idea of what is being experienced, and what the experience does is to "fill out" the nature of the teaching already received. For example, when St. Paul had his life-shattering Damascus road experience, it was unexpected, confusing, and yet consonant with all that had preceded it. On the one hand, it was an experience that destroyed his previous beliefs about Jesus Christ and his followers. Yet, on the other hand, we can perhaps surmise that it was in line with his deep-seated thoughts about the strange man from Nazareth and thus led to a devastating rearrangement of his theology. It was, therefore, not totally surprising.

But we need to be sure that religious experience is in fact the experience of meeting an objective God and not simply that of wish fulfillment. The idea that "if you believe a thing hard enough, it will happen" is not unknown in history. Honesty compels us to acknowledge that we have no real objective way of knowing. We have to realize that other people's experiences are totally inaccessible to us, are all the really deep, intimate moments of life when they occur to others. If someone says to me, "I am in love with this adorable girl!" I have to accept his word that there is a reality to his awed words, flushed expression, and wide eyes. That it could be put down to indigestion is a possibility—but I would be a cynic to suspect this has to be the case at first appearance, unless I know he suffers from indigestion!

Some time ago I led a conference in New Zealand and spoke to a lady in her fifties, a well-educated and thoughtful woman who sadly was in perpetual pain with a degenerative spinal problem and who had problems of depression. I met her again a few weeks later and she was clearly a different person. She told me that she was healed. Her back was normal—according to her doctor—and her mental attitude was obviously better. She was so much better that I even doubted at first if this was the woman I had talked and prayed with earlier. Her claim was that, through my prayers and through a healing conference she attended, she was now wholly better through the direct intervention of the Holy Spirit. She was now whole. I was overjoyed to see this, but I must admit that at the time my innate skepticism clashed with my conviction that God can and does heal today. But when he does, we are astounded and dumbfounded—even those of us who should not be! We get somehow nervous when we stumble on the frightening fact—as it surely is—that God is personally at work in the world today. But how could I be sure that what she was claiming was the truth? Further investigation confirmed the woman's story; she was infinitely better and her friends vouched for the startling return to full health in body and mind. However, I had no access to the actual experience that led to that healing. Now I return to my question, "How could I be sure that it was an experience of God?" Yes, I could have jumped to the conclusion that the experience of healing was due to wish fulfillment, but I find that explanation, in this lady's case, far more unconvincing than that God's power was directly at work within her, restoring her to full health.

It seems that there are no tests to check on such claims if, that is, the claims of others cannot be verified for certain. However, while there are no objective scientific tests we can apply, there are, as we shall see, some observations that will assist us in discerning whether the claim is true or false. But before we consider that, we must outline the main types of religious experience and note what they have meant to the individuals concerned.

Within the Christian tradition the experience of God has taken many different forms. Down the centuries people have claimed to have met God in a variety of ways, which, for them, have been unique and life-changing. We can, however, distinguish five main forms.

First of all, one type focuses on "sight," whether or not the experience has been physical or spiritual. Some have claimed to have actually "seen" God. This type of experience is frequent in Scripture; we think of Abraham and the angelic

beings who meet and talk with him; we think of St. Paul and
his vision of God, which resulted in blindness and eventual
restoration of sight. But this experience is not confined to the
covers of sacred history. It has also been claimed by many
down the centuries and in our own day. The appearances of
the Virgin Mary claimed to have been seen by many at the
Yugoslavian town of Medjugorje belong to this type. It is
difficult for those of us who have never had a visual encounter
with spiritual reality to know how to react to such claims. For
the moment we must suspend judgment and listen to the
stories that people tell of their meeting with the numinous.

There is another type of experience that, while less direct,
is no less vivid and meaningful to the recipient. This is where
people have encountered the presence of God through
dreams and sensory experiences, which have led to the
accounts of being "overwhelmed" or "enveloped" by God.
Dr. F.C. Happold describes in his book *Religious Faith and
Twentieth Century Man* the story of his own experience: "It
happened in my room in Peterhouse in the evening of 1
February 1913, when I was an undergraduate at Cambridge.
If I say Christ came to me I should be using conventional
words which would carry no precise meaning; for Christ
comes to men and women in different ways. When I tried to
record the experience at the time I used the imagery of the
Holy Grail; it seemed to me to be just like that. There was,
however, no sensible vision. There was just the room, with
its shabby furniture and the red shaded lamp on the table. But
the room was filled with a Presence, which in a strange way
was both about me and within me, like light or warmth. I was

overwhelmingly possessed by Someone who was not myself, and yet I felt I was more myself than I had ever been before. I was filled with an intense happiness, an almost unbearable joy, such as I had never known before and never known since. And over all was a deep sense of peace and security and certainty. Some experiences of this sort, which I have found recorded, lasted a very short time. Mine lasted several hours . . ." The actress Sarah Miles also stated in a Press interview that she had been converted from atheism by mystical experiences of this sort that overwhelmed her for no apparent reason.

We note that the "reality" of the two types of experiences we have just considered is conveyed through sensory perception. Happold, for example, resists the idea that it was a direct visual encounter in his room, but he is equally sure that the entire meeting was real and, we might say, sacramental. This raises the question about the relationship between material and spiritual realities. Somehow what people are struggling to convey is the way in which the ordinary is transfused, as well as transformed, by the divine presence. Remarkably, St. Augustine, that great philosopher and possibly the first great psychologist, described his conversion in ways that recall the five senses; he heard, saw, smelled, tasted, and touched God—or was it not all along the case that God took the initiative and encountered him? So he wrote, "You called to me, you cried aloud to me, you broke my barrier of deafness. You shone upon me, your radiancy enveloped me. You put my blindness to flight. You shed your fragrance about me. I drew breath and I gasp for your sweet odour. I tasted you and

I hunger and thirst for you. You touched me and I am inflamed with love of your peace."

Third, there are experiences that many Christians have had where the experience of meeting God has resulted in a state of peace, well-being, or calm awareness of God's presence. Here are two illustrations taken from different traditions: "I was kneeling one evening in the quietness of the chapel before the Blessed sacrament as my habit was," wrote a Roman Catholic lady, "when a deep and contented peace came upon me. I had the strange sensation that I was not alone; that someone was with me. An indescribable feeling of joy and happiness welled up within me. I was so glad—my heart seemed to be bursting with delight at his presence. When I left the chapel after what seemed such a brief and wonderful time, I discovered I had been there for two and a half hours!" From a different tradition within the church a young man narrates his experience in the following way: "I was in my second year at Oxford University and had been going to church for a few months. I was not much of a church-goer, to be honest, but one evening I went and listened to a lively sermon that made me aware of the claims of Christ on my life. I went back to my lodgings convinced of the reality of the Christian faith. The preacher had spoken about asking Jesus into your life. Not quite sure what this meant, I sat on my bed and thought about it and realized that I wanted to be a full-blooded Christian. So, in the quietness of my room, I prayed that God would accept me. I can't claim that I heard a voice or anything like that. I just felt that I wasn't talking to the ceiling but that I was accepted. Christianity was now real for me.

Into the category of the experience of God's presence we can put John Wesley's conversion when he felt "my heart was strangely warmed." Surely that must be the understatement of all time! Wesley's meeting with God that evening not only changed a disillusioned missionary into a man of conviction, but it spearheaded a religious and social revolution in the eighteenth century and led to millions sharing that life-changing event. The testimonies of the young man and John Wesley are, of course, common to the great evangelical tradition where commitment to the Christian revelation is said to be sealed through a heart experience of God's love and his forgiveness through the cross.

A fourth type we might call "encounter" experiences, which focus on ways in which people encounter the "otherness," the "numinous," the "mysteriousness" of God. Two influential thinkers, Martin Buber, a Jewish philosopher, and Rudolph Otto, a German Protestant theologian, have shown how prevalent the experience of meeting God is in human life. It may happen through what Otto called the experience of *mysterium tremendum,* by which he meant an experience of God through nature, in art, and so on, where feelings of awe and wonder may be compared to Moses' encounter with God at the burning bush. Or a meeting with God might come in a mystical experience leading to a realization of the holiness and majesty of almighty God (well-documented testimony down the Christian centuries). But it might, conceivably, come through the intervention of God at points of despair, illness, and even at the point of death. Experiences of healing are seen by many as direct intervention by a creator God who has revealed himself personally and lovingly in some specific way. Those of us with extensive pastoral experience do not need to be reminded of the frequency of such claims and, interestingly, it often happens to those outside the formal structures of the Christian faith as well as to those within it.

Finally, we must point to that "experience" of even more people that is the quiet testimony of God's providential dealings with them in life. They may have encountered tragedy, difficulty, and pain (indeed, often such ingredients are part of the testimony itself) and they point to God's hand in delivering them or interpreting the pain or problem. While this is scarcely "experience" in a direct way—indeed, some believers might be reticent about claiming it as an experience at all—it is experience of a faith that is for them authentic and relevant. The ordered world of daily business, family life, and daily prayer, the influence of impressive Christian living by others, the importance of the sacraments in worship and so on, are contexts in which such people find God's presence in their lives. For such people, there is hardly a need for extraordinary interventions because God is with them all the time.

We must, however, at this point make a most important observation. The character of Christian experience of God encompasses much more than certain individuals having had experiences of him. The church itself is founded upon the experience of those who have met God and whose lives have been changed as a result. It is highly doubtful that there would have been such an institution as the church if the first disciples had not witnessed the resurrection and believed down to the last fiber of their beings that they had met God. It is, furthermore, extremely unlikely that Saul the Rabbi would have given up such an interesting and career-fulfilling occupation as persecuting Christians unless a real event—for him—on the Damascus road had not put an end to it and led him outside the religious establishment of his day. It is highly doubtful, also, if the missionary enterprise of the church down the ages would have got off the ground at all if the saints, martyrs, and missionaries had not experienced their own sense of God's personal "call." All these experiences, and many more besides, can hardly be shrugged off as irrelevant to our quest for God. Indeed, we have to grant that experience is at the heart of the Christian faith. To know God is to know him, not as an article in the creed, but as a real person. If, then, God is real and is the One behind all things that are, we are not surprised to hear a testimony rising from the hearts of many people that he does disclose himself and the hem of his garment may be touched. And we must be clear about that— that is all that such experiences are. No experience of God is really a revealing of the whole God in all his splendor and majesty. At the best, we catch but glimpses of his nature and grace.

But how do we test the reality of such experiences? What *are* we to make of such claims? We must obviously start with the character of the person who is claiming an experience of meeting God. Who is this person who tells me of the God he has encountered? Is she a person I respect and trust? Does the testimony ring true to what I know of her, her intellect, moral standing, temperament, and character? The more sane, rational, and well known to me an individual is, the more likely I am to accept what she has to say. I may not be prepared to believe yet what she believes, or to follow her way, but I will not be able to deny that for her the experience of knowing God has resulted in something that has challenged her previous way of handling life and challenges mine as well. What I will not be able to get at will be the actual experience itself—but, as we acknowledged earlier, that is true of any personal claim or conviction whether it be religious or secular. What I can do is view that experience in the context of this person's life. If a basically sane and rational man or woman whose life and character is invariably well-integrated actually claims to have had such an experience, then I may be impressed and even deeply disconcerted—and may have to revise my ideas about God and how he works.

Second, we must apply the test of moral consequences. If someone claims to have experienced the living God we will not expect him or her to carry on as if it is of no significance. We will want to ask: "What difference has it made to his or her life?" For example, some years ago I had as a student a most interesting man who became a Christian in prison. This man, David, was sentenced to ten years for a serious kidnapping offense. He was a very nasty customer. In prison he was brought to his senses through the break-up of his marriage, a realization of the stupidity of his life and its lack of moral direction. Over a period of time he opened his mind and heart to God. One evening, the culmination of many months of discussing and arguing with a prison visitor, he cried out in despair in the quietness of his cell: "I am hopeless, rotten, and in need. If you are real, God, reveal yourself to me." That was the turning point, David was to say later, and he quietly claims that God met him that night in a personal way that made him a different man. There was nothing spectacular about this, but there is little doubt that, for David, it was a life-changing event. And this is what we should expect if an experience of meeting God is real—it will result in a changed life, in different habits, and a revolutionized lifestyle.

So, we might say, one way of checking the truth or falsity of such claims to have "seen," "met," or "heard" God is by what we may call a "reality check" on the lives of those who make such statements about claims to know God. While a person's more skeptical friends may doubt the value of his arguments about the truth of the Christian faith, the *reality* of his faith and his testimony to the power of God in his life will not be something they can quickly ignore or reject.

Nevertheless it must be concluded that experience itself is not a conclusive argument for the existence of God. That is not what I am arguing. After all, there are people of other faiths or none at all who have had mystical experiences and we can't all be right! And, of course, a Christian would not want to claim that one religious experience solves all of life's problems. We do not see experience standing on its own in any sense. Experience must have the support of argument if it is to convince. Just as faith without works is dead, so experience without a strong grounding in a biblical faith, together with a rational framework, is dead also. The value of experience for many people is twofold; first, it reorders into a coherent whole what up to now in a person's life has been disparate and unorganized. Many have testified that through the experience of meeting God, their hearts and minds have found what they have been seeking and yearning for for years.

Second, we must clearly understand that experience is not a special kind of truth, nor is religious experience a queer, unnatural kind of experience belonging to some strange and other world. Experience of God is encountered in ordinary life and we may describe it as ordinary experience understood at full depth. What makes that truth religious is not that it relates to some abnormal field of thought and feeling, but that it goes to the very root of the experience that it interprets. T.S. Eliot's evocative words, "We had the experience but missed the meaning" go to the very center of modern life. Openness to God enables the ordinary experiences of life to become fully impregnated with meaning and divine reality.

Experience, then, undergirds faith and reason. It can never replace them. But for the person who up to now has been reflecting on the Christian faith, the invitation comes "to taste and see that the Lord is good." There can be no denying that the variegated experiences of God are powerful challenges to modern secular people; their philosophy of "seeing is believing" is confounded by a form of experiencing that has had such a powerful influence upon people down the centuries and still continues to do so today.

8

The Case against Unbelief

WE SAID AT THE BEGINNING OF THIS BOOK THAT FAITH IS not given a real opportunity in Western culture to present its case for a living and loving God because the entire weight of opinion and culture stifles its voice and does not pay heed to its message. The confident message that comes across is that Christianity is discredited and that, regretfully, its story belongs to the past along with other myths of perfection and life everlasting. We are being robbed of a chance to discover the reality of a firm faith in God and of encountering him as creator and friend. But, really, is it a fact that faith has had its day?

If that is the case, we have to ask why it has persisted in maintaining a stubborn presence in the Marxist-Leninist culture of the Soviet Union, China, and other places where deliberate attempts have been made to squeeze it out of existence. Indeed, its resurgence in places where atheistic communism has suppressed Christianity for decades is an impressive story. And it is a matter of wonder that it still continues to exist and flourish in the sophisticated, technological cultures of the West where, although leaner and slimmer since Christianity has separated from its secular culture, it is perhaps more effective than it has ever been because of its stand upon issues of morality and value, matters that continue to meet an echo in the aspirations of modern people.

It is my conviction that rather than faith in a personal God being intellectually discredited, the reverse is the case. It is not that modern science has found Christian belief to be lacking an intellectual basis but, rather, when all the facts are considered together we begin to see atheism, unbelief, and materialism as the impostors they are. In this chapter I want to explore the serious weaknesses of atheistic materialism and to show that far from presenting a threat to faith, the questions it cannot answer tip the balance in favor of the hypothesis of God.

First, materialism is *unconvincing.* We are asked to believe that sheer chance brought the entire universe into existence. We are also told that we must not posit the existence of a personal God because that hypothesis is unprovable anyway. Instead we are exhorted to marvel at the great god "Chance" who created all things. But when the facts are considered together, we have grounds to be skeptical of such a theory.

Let us look at the evidence. We are asked to believe that a totally random event, the famous "Big Bang," created the universe as we know it, which led to the creation of matter and time. We are asked further to accept another thesis that, unplanned, out of the primeval soup of amino acids, organic life emerged and, millions of years later, intelligent life appeared.

In the last decade or so scientists have taken a special interest in chance and have applied scientific data to the laws of probability—the results to date have shaken scientific thinking. Professor Bartholomew of London University asks, for example, how order can arise out of primeval chaos when the stream of development is running in the opposite direction. That is to say, when chaos is supposed to have been the original characteristic of primeval creation it is surprising that conditions to support life emerged. He and many other scientists have shown that rather than order arising by "accident" from chaos, it was there in the first place, that the distribution of gas in the universe from the "big bang" had to be delicately and precisely balanced to produce galaxies, and that even an error of minute proportions $(1:10^{40})$ would have destroyed life. We are left, therefore, startled at the "miracle" of this chance event. Bartholomew wonders whether this suggests rather that "there must have been a deliberate input of information at an early stage which served as a program (in the computing sense) to engineer the highly-structured world we live in."

A similar problem emerges from the chance of life starting from the primeval soup of amino acids (which are thought to be at the origin of life). We are told that over a period of billions of years the random mixing of these acids spontaneously generated life. Most of us happily accept these facts because the information comes to us with the *imprimatur* of science, assuring us that the facts are infallibly correct. Yet the odds against this happening of its own volition are simply huge. Hoyle and Asoka J. Wickrema Sinha (a biochemist) have postulated that the probability of creating 2,000 highly complex enzymes from random combinations of amino acids is infinitesimal. Hoyle likens it to the same odds as throwing an uninterrupted sequence of 50,000 sixes with unbiased dice. Sure, it could happen over millions of years, but the odds involved are simply fantastic. And all this, mind you, precedes the astonishing appearance of intelligent life on an obscure little planet in the backwaters of the universe.

However, it is important not to overplay the argument from probability. Bartholomew, in a restrained and considered essay, subjects the hypothesis of Hoyle and Wickrema Sinha to critical analysis and shows that such enormous odds quoted do not prove God beyond reasonable doubt. And this is quite true. All it reveals is the staggering odds involved in postulating intelligent life originating spontaneously without the direct will of a creator. But what is significant is that the case for materialism, resting as it does on random happenings, on unintelligent and accidental causes, has now to face the fact that the odds of the world we know and intelligent life emerging are overwhelmingly huge. Consider the implications of the remarks of the scientist Mark Doughty who explains that in the very first milliseconds after the original explosion there must have been present all the conditions for life on our seemingly insignificant planet, including the self-directed and self-conscious form of life that we call human, and that our human brains were encoded in certain minute atomic data present at the dawn of time. Little wonder that the idea of a creator who planned the universe seems to most people to be more plausible than a materialistic explanation. The philosopher Swinburne comments with some force: "It is very unlikely that a universe would exist uncaused but rather more likely that God would exist uncaused." For Swinburne, and many of us, the explanation of the universe is made more puzzling, not less, by the denial of a personal creator.

Second, materialism is *unlikely*. Let me use a rather rough analogy. If we were told that the first typewriter was, in fact, not the product of intelligence but fashioned haphazardly and randomly by forces of nature, in which the different parts came together over millions of years—each piece undesigned, and undifferentiated—finally arriving at comprising a product that is intelligible, some credulity would be required for us to accept this idea, which goes completely against our experience of life. We would marvel at such a process and probably suspect the presence of a mind to bring this about. Of course, we are not opposed to the idea of evolution over millions of years. Most of us accept that hypothesis. But what I am skeptical of is the suggestion that random events can produce the order we see around us. And let us make no mistake about it. As we argued earlier, the very order of the universe is such an overwhelming fact that it not only creates the possibility for knowledge and science, but also is part of the condition of an intelligent universe. As Professor Farmer put it so splendidly years ago: "It is only because the fire can be relied on to boil the kettle, and the sound waves to carry our speech, that we can indulge in that highly personal activity called a tea-party."

What we are arguing for here is continuity between the universe and ourselves. For the materialist, intelligence, consciousness, illusions of freedom, and so on are but the epiphenomenon that is a by-product of life. They have no existence apart from us and are but accidental additions that have arisen by good fortune. This suggestion, with whatever sophistication it is expressed, is *desperate*, because to be convincing it has to deny not only our experience of life—which we assume to be logical and intelligent—but it also has to sever consciousness and intelligence from life by making them elements that are by-products of impersonal and mechanistic forces; they are merely the concomitants of certain types of organic life. They exist in us and nowhere else. But we have to ask with the Catholic philosopher Lonergan, how it is that this world and all we experience may be interpreted by intelligence if it does not have an intelligent basis? How curious it is that in all our exploring, searching, and struggling we find that our minds meet a Mind. The physicist David Bohm concluded that materialism left more questions unanswered than it solved and remarked: "When I see the immense order of the universe (and especially the brain of man) I cannot escape feeling that this ground unfolds supreme intelligence. And although this is not quite so evident, I would say that this intelligence is permeated with compassion and love."

Third, materialism is *limiting*. Exclude God from life and allow that all morality and standards of value are relative because God is not, and the result is not greater freedom for humankind but a fresh bondage because our spirits are now chained. The irony is that we need God to be fully human. Materialism, instead of revealing the true character of life, obscures it because it mistakes mystery for superstition. But mystery is necessary if humankind is to grow to its full stature. Strangely enough, science and philosophy are beginning to acknowledge that the only way we can have a true and full understanding of the universe is in terms of analogy, meta-phor, poetry, and sometimes paradox. Niels Bohr, the emi-nent quantum physicist, is forced, for example, in his discipline to resort to metaphor when he describes scientific truth in the following way: "When it comes to atoms, language can be used only as in poetry. The poet (like the quantum physicist) is concerned with creating images and establishing connections . . . Quantum theory provides us with a striking illustration of the fact that we can fully understand a connec-tion though we can only speak of it in images and parables."

But scientists, in drawing upon metaphor and poetry to describe things that are beyond sensory perception, are also being compelled to reject a materialism that was at the heart of a nineteenth-century philosophy of science. David Bohm argues that it is a mistake to regard the elemental particles of matter as "things" that collectively make up bigger things. This "building block" method is dismissed. Rather we should think of the world as a "network of relations." Our experience of it may be as a collection of "things," but to the quantum scientist it is an integrated web of energy patterns in which nothing is independent. Bohm is led to the conclusion that "The implicate order implies a reality immensely beyond matter. Matter itself is merely a ripple in this background—and the ocean of energy is not primarily in space or time at all." This way of looking at reality opens up the one-dimensional universe of materialism and makes it possible for us to see the wonderful mystery of life and the way that science, art, philosophy, poetry, and human living each has its part to play in illuminating life and its richness. Professor Stuart Hampshire similarly attacks materialism for its reductionism: "Materialism is wrong because it does not do justice to the mental life in terms of imagination, belief, and memory and to its social implications."

It is this rejection of a cosmic Mind and of a divine purpose that is at the heart of materialism. For many decades it has reigned supreme because it seems so completely and literally "sensible." There did not seem to be any real reason to go beyond the evidences of the physical world to explain the whole of reality. But these days there are very few physicists who would claim to be clear materialists or empiricists. The reason for this is twofold. The first has to do with the nature of reality. We no longer believe in the old "billiard ball" idea of nature but in a complex structure of things that makes the older way of seeing things difficult to accept today. The mechanical world of Newtonian physics—according to which all things that exist are physical things with a distinct reality, however small they may be—gave way to an Einsteinian universe in which this description was abandoned. Leptons, quarks, muons, and photons are not pieces of matter in any imaginable sense. Eddington used to give an example of the two different approaches when in lectures he spoke of his two tables. The first was solid, brown, three feet high and rectangular and quite obviously visible. The other was mostly space with here and there some mysterious entity that had to be imagined at one moment as a wave and at another as a particle. As Eddington made clear, these did not represent two different tables but the same reality—and both were correct from different perceptions. In short, the great attraction of materialism led to its downfall. It appeared to be the case that the only fundamental properties of the structure of things are mass, position, and velocity. But modern physics has not so much destroyed the old mechanistic view of the universe as it has made it seem too superficial. We now see the universe as a vastly more mysterious and complex entity than the former "billiard ball" view of things.

The second reason has to do with the way that materialism separates life into two great compartments. The first is the physical world; cold, indifferent, and hostile to humanity. The second is the world of culture and life we create to sustain ourselves, which is warm, friendly, and meaningful up to a point. Quite obviously, the disjuncture of these two realities reveals a failure on the part of materialism to give a real basis for human life, values, and morals but, given its starting point, how can it relate the two worlds if the former is the harsh reality of all things and the latter the accidental by-product of impersonal forces in nature? So it appears that such forms of materialism are unsatisfactory because they open up a chasm between life of the world and human culture and aspirations. A coherent philosophy and science must do justice to both worlds.

Fourth, materialistic atheism is *unsatisfactory in its understanding of value*. We all know the problem of evil for the Christian. Our chapter earlier did not minimize the questions posed by affirming God's love, which is daily challenged by disasters and events that make us ask what God is doing. But by focussing the searchlight on the believer, the person who rejects God may be oblivious of the uncomfortable questions that search him out, perhaps even more rigorously. First, prevalent as evil most certainly is in the world, who needs convincing that the presence of good far outweighs the element of evil? Harmony, peace, goodness, hope, joy, and love are the basic constituents of life more than evil, destruction, and death. Such realities are the bases of the great civilizations; they flood our literature and illuminate our homes and lives; they give meaning and stability.

Furthermore, if there is no God, no final explanation of this world, it is incumbent upon us to explain the problem of good in a godless world. Adolph Deissmann once remarked: "You should never take anything away from a person unless you can give him something better." We are still awaiting this better world view from the non-believer. How do we reconcile with a blind, indifferent, and irrational cosmos, the discovery of truth, beauty, and the power of sacrificial love? The majority of us just cannot accept the notion that such virtues are culturally formed and governed. Whether we are practicing Christians or not, the presence of moral values and human values of grace and dignity are seen by many of us as pointing beyond us to a "Something" or "Someone" who transcends us and calls us to a "divinity" we do not as yet possess. Our god-idea is the acid test of our valuation of life. As we saw earlier, the moral framework of life is shattered or severely weakened when the faith around it, on which it was built, is destroyed. Atheism destroys the basis of any kind of moral certainty. But when we take the issue of freedom, the atheist is particularly vulnerable. It is a feature of existential atheism to reject God, on the one hand—to make room for human freedom on the belief that the existence of God destroys the autonomy and freedom of mankind. Yet, on the other hand, the same philosophy will reject belief in God because he does not intervene to rescue the victims of human villainy! Atheists cannot have it both ways.

But let us go deeper into this question of value. It is of course possible for the unbeliever to argue that our total concepts of morality and human goodness are but the random products of physical events, that claims of religious experience are illusory, and that humankind's pleasure in art, music, and things of the spirit do not point beyond him but come from his deepest aspirations only. But the net result is to take from life the very things that give to it its significance and meaning. So the writer Philip Toynbee comments: "What I would say is that if it were irrefutably demonstrated to me that there is no God, and no reality above or distinct from the material world, then I would consider that human life is too

terrible to be endured. Fear and some regard for the feelings
of others might prevent me killing myself but I would live out
my life as a prisoner." Toynbee is giving expression to feelings
that many of us have about the value of the transcendent in
life. It is not that God is called upon to be a Father-substitute
to face a hostile world, but that we perceive that we cannot
conceive of morality and such values as freedom, love, peace,
and hope without addressing a Being who gives these qualities their authentication. The position of the theist is that in
moral awareness and the growth of conscience we trace the
mark of God the Creator, who has created us in such a way
that we are aware of how we should live and behave—in a
good and loving way. We call these discoveries "moral dis-
closures" because they point from us to a God who has made
us in his image and likeness.

Enough has been written in this chapter to suggest that the
Christian concept of a personal God is superior to ideas that
reject him. I believe strongly that belief in a personal God has
advantages over agnosticism and atheism in the following
respects:

1. By believing in the existence of a rational and personal
creator we have a more *comprehensive* picture of the
universe. It is a universe with a purposeful and loving
creator who is working out his plan for all things in the
vicissitudes and trials of life. A non-theistic explanation, as
we have seen, has the difficulty of explaining how order
came from disorder (if that is the case) and, if order was
the primary reality, how that came into existence. Agnos-

ticism only projects its agnosticism further back. More questions have to be answered if God is rejected. A theistic explanation does not believe that agnosticism is justified and suggests that the most reasonable hypothesis is that the primary reality is a creator God who has brought all things into being.

2. We argue, furthermore, that theism is a more *simple and satisfactory* explanation. We are used to making and creating things, and it is reasonable to deduce that, in a world in which order and causality reign, a personal act willed that the universe should have this character. Although this explanation is simple and straightforward, the understanding of reality and the way it takes us into analogy, metaphor, and mystery is far from being simplistic. The history of Christian thought is a sufficient denial of the idea that to be a Christian believer means crucifying one's intellect. On the contrary, such a faith integrates knowledge and experience; it awakens awe, mystery, and wonder, which are at the heart of being a human being.

3. The presence of a personal creator *makes sense* of our place in the scheme of things and *unites* the world of nature and humankind, which atheism divides. Instead of seeing ourselves as exceptional beings, creatures curiously and inextricably thrown up by chance in a mysterious cosmos, we see the unity of everything and, in this way, can see the principle of morality that stands over us and beckons us to fullness of life. The statement of the scientist,

Freeman Dyson, quoted earlier, that "the universe in some sense must have known we were coming" coincides with the Christian conviction that this created order is truly our home and the place where we meet God.

9

What Kind of God?

WE HAVE SEEN THAT THERE ARE REASONABLE GROUNDS FOR postulating the existence of a Being who has created all things. Some people, however, want us to stop there with an unknowable, ultimately mysterious divinity who is inaccessible to us. They remind us of the vastness of this wonderful universe and tell us that such immensities mock our feeble attempts to communicate with the creator. We must go no further, they tell us. We must live with mystery. "Yes, we grant that the clues for the existence of God are strong but nothing more can be said. Be content with the little we know."

We can make two responses to this call for agnosticism. First, it hardly seems logical to make the vastness of the universe an obstacle to God communicating his essence to us. To affirm that God exists is to say, as we have pointed out, that this universe is not a product of blind chance but is controlled by an intelligent purpose. It does not make sense, therefore, to say he exists but that he has no plans for us and he keeps himself aloof from his creation. If he is able to contemplate the great details of creation, he is surely able to give personal attention to the intimate details of life. It follows from the nature of a supreme being that it is precisely because he is supreme that he is able to care about small things. We reduce God to our likeness when we doubt his power to reveal himself.

Of course we should realize that God in his essence is ultimately beyond our full understanding. We talk about God as "he" but must appreciate that such language is only analogical. God is "wholly other." When the Bible uses the masculine pronoun "he," and when it also uses both masculine and feminine attributes to describe God, it is unlikely that such terminology was intended to be taken as literally true, even by the writers of sacred literature. This is to say, then, that such images must not be taken literally as suggesting that God is "male." Whatever we say about the creator only approximates to "his" nature. "We see through a glass darkly" is true of all Christian thought. Though we may be confident about our knowledge of God, his greatness is ultimately beyond our thinking and conceiving. Perhaps we in the West, then, need to learn from the tradition of Eastern Orthodoxy, which approaches the mystery of God by the way of negativity in order to understand the wonder of the One who has given us life. This *via negativa* starts by saying what

God is not, in order to arrive at what he is for us. Sometimes called "kataphatic" theology, the method of the East moves from negation to a cautious knowledge of God who is unchanging, not limited, all-loving, and so on. This type of approach is caught beautifully in the poet R.S. Thomas's description of God:

> Why no! I never thought other than
> That God is the great absence
> In our lives, the empty silence
> Within, the place where we go
> Seeking, not in hope to
> Arrive or find.
> He keeps the interstices
> In our knowledge, the darkness
> Between stars.
> His are the echoes
> We follow, the footprints he has
> just Left.

This stance, which starts with the greatness of God, is a healthy corrective to the confident assumptions of the tradition of Western Christianity, which has often too brashly assumed that God's nature is self-evident and that we can make clear dogmatic statements about him. The danger of this approach (which has been called the "apophatic" tradition), is that we make God into an object of knowledge and lose sight of his majesty and awesome might. Nevertheless, a balanced idea of God will contain both these emphases; we do exist in God and his world, and in this life we shall never be able to penetrate beyond the outer courtyard of knowledge, but he is still a Father, friend, and redeemer to those who trust him.

If our first response to agnosticism, then, must spring from our understanding of God's ability to give attention to everything, always, and all at once, the second response must flow from the character of God as one whose nature is always to give. Revelation springs from "giving." To give is to reveal what was formerly hidden. We have many illustrations of this from everyday life. When someone gives himself or herself to me in acts of sacrifice, generosity, and love, something new is shared that comes with the gift—a revelation of the love-gift. Similarly, by creating, God pours his very self into his creation and comes to us. This means that the creator has made it possible for us to receive these intimations of the divine. The Jewish theologian J. Neusner speaks splendidly of "man's walled mind which has no access to a ladder upon which he can, on his own strength, rise to knowledge of God. Yet his soul is endowed with translucent windows that open to the beyond." Even though Christian theology correctly questions humankind's ability to discern fully the work of God in his world through our fallenness, yet we are not always blind to the wonder of his works or deaf to his call. Some of us have experienced those moments of translucence when we have caught a glimpse of the beauty of nature with such intensity that we have wanted to exclaim with Gerard Hopkins, "the world is charged with the grandeur of God!" Hopkins's poem goes on to affirm the "dearest, freshness deep down things" of God's creation. For others, the awareness of the spiritual has come through the awesome media of music, poetry, or art. In a million different ways the giving of God goes on and our antennae have the ability to pick up the signals of a universal God who reveals himself in the music and poetry of creation. It is no accident, then, that we can "hear" the language of God because the facility has been given to us.

We can go much further than that. We have to say that a Christian is not a philosopher who has found a satisfactory theory of the universe but is someone who believes in a personal God. One cannot pray to an abstraction but only to a person. So, the cry of the Christian thinker Paul Claudel on the evening of his conversion to the Christian faith as he stood by a pillar in the cathedral of Notre Dame was: "Lord, all of a sudden you have become for me a person!" Christians are not people who have discovered a useful world view, or an interesting and absorbing philosophy, or a caring lifestyle—although we would submit that it is all and more of these things. Christians are a body of followers of Jesus Christ who have life, hope, and purpose through him. He is alive and lives in them.

If, in creating, the giving of God is known, we also find in this giving a self-limitation on the part of God. It is normal in Christian theology to talk about God as omniscient and omnipotent. But is he in fact all-powerful? This traditional way of talking about God hardly makes sense when full rein is given to the fact of his self-giving. By creating individuals with free will, God himself is limited by his act of creation; he chooses to be diminished in order for us to grow. We do not diminish him but he freely and deliberately enters upon a process of self-emptying (kenosis) and refrains from using his power. He creates a world in which we have freedom to grow; a freedom that entails the risk that part of his creation may reject him, abuse his freedom, exploit his world, and even usurp the powers of the creator. So close is divinization and demonization; the brave new world so quickly becomes the killing fields of man's greed and hatred.

It is because of this link between God's self-giving and self-limitation that I for one am grateful for the insights of a theological movement known as "process theology." Two thinkers in particular have popularized this new way of looking at God's ways with his creation—the mathematician Alfred Whitehead and the philosopher Charles Hartshorne. Process theology rejects the idea of God as being totally "outside time" and as an immutable Being—that is, unchangeable in his nature. They accuse traditional theology of failing to do justice to the rich biblical portrait of God who suffers with his creation and they charge it with absorbing concepts of an unchanging God that owe more to Greek thought than Christian ideas. Process thought sees the whole of creation as being "in process," with God being immanent and transcendent. In his immanence God works within the process of creation and to some degree is subject to the laws that are fundamental to its existence. Thus in contrast with traditional views of God, which see him outside events, process theology envisages the creator as being influenced by events.

There is much that is attractive about process thought. It makes sense of a world that is plainly in process. "The creation waits in eager expectation for the sons of God to be revealed" is how St. Paul saw a universe on its way to full redemption (Romans 8, NIV). The same passage shows God's close involvement with his creation in suffering with it and caring for it and bringing it to eventual rebirth. Process theology is coherent in speaking of a creator so intimately associated with his workmanship that he is also affected by it. He takes suffering and change into himself and transforms them into hopeful possibilities of growth. From this perspective, evil itself can be considered to be redemptive, because if God is in the processes of life and is affected by them, nothing is totally and irredeemably evil. Such a description of God in relation to his world is surely deeply Christian. God remains God but always with his creation, rejoicing in its achievements and suffering from its failures. Christianity, with its doctrine of the incarnation, will identify with any beliefs about God that "earth" him in the reality of the world.

There are several aspects of process theology, however, that make me hesitate in embracing it wholeheartedly. There is, on the one hand, a tendency on the part of some process theologians to create a philosophy of process thought that has but tenuous connections with Christian thought. Thus, Whitehead's model of God with its "primordial" and "consequent" poles (which is his attempt to replace the classical modes of immanence and transcendence) is scarcely obvious. On what basis do we reject the one as being non-Christian and yet accept the other? But, more seriously, so

completely does this theology subsume God within his creation that it appears to make him a creature of time, seemingly
impotent to deal with the problems of life. The problem, then,
for process theology appears to be that of its failure to balance
immanence with the transcendence of God. Unless God is
seen as standing outside the structures, we will end up with
a God who is imprisoned by his own laws.

Nevertheless, process thought is right in what it affirms of
God's involvement in life, and this concept of God is thoroughly biblical and takes us directly into the character of God
as revealed by Scripture. In defining what God is like, the
Bible gives us many possible answers, which range from his
transcendence over all things as a loving Creator to the one
who comes to us in humility in a human life. Now, although
the Bible is, for the Christian, God's clearest testimony of who
he is and what he demands from us, it is also the record of
humankind's search for God and his gradual self-revelation.
We find in the Old Testament, for example, men and women
groping beyond themselves for the divine and finding him
little by little. To a great extent the picture of God developed
as people discovered him and as he made them his people.
Indeed, there is a curious overlapping of revelation and
searching. The knowledge of God came from God's side as
he allowed his people to see different facets of his character.
Yet from another point of view, they "discovered" him as their
pilgrimage continued. Through the *acts* of God they found
the true God. So Abraham is led out by the Unknown into a
new land and each act of faith is rewarded by fresh revelations
of the One who goes before.

Similarly, the events that happened to the Hebrew tribes in Egypt—and their subsequent escape—proceed from their risk of faith and lead them into knowledge of the One who declares himself to be *Yahweh,* the One who is Eternal, yet ever present. The high point of knowledge of God is found in the great prophetic tradition that finds its peak in Isaiah, Jeremiah, Hosea, and Amos. Here God is splendidly depicted as the Creator of all things, the One who has no rival. Isaiah supplies the grandeur of a lofty deity, Jeremiah the highly personal qualities of One who cares, while Hosea and Amos add the ingredient that such a God makes ethical demands upon people that coincide with his character as one who loves, who is pure and holy.

The New Testament does not contradict the development of the Old Testament, but it does add something quite unusual, controversial and, for the Christian, wonderful: namely that the human face of God is Jesus Christ. He, claims the New Testament, is the way to the Father.

But did Jesus himself make this claim? The answer appears somewhat ambiguous when we go directly to the earliest gospels written. The synoptic Gospels, that is, Matthew, Mark and Luke, reveal a reticence on the part of Jesus to be explicit about himself and his mission. Jesus makes few claims for himself, but draws them from his disciples. "Who do people say I am?" drew various responses from his followers. One of them was: "Some say you are a prophet, even as great as Elijah." And then the swift counterpunch: "And what about you? Who do you think I am?" This evoked Simon Peter's famous confession: "You are the Christ (Messiah), the Son of the living God." It is arguably the case that, although this confession was a watershed in the disciples' understanding of Jesus, uncertainty and mystery still clouded him. It was not until after his death and resurrection that clarity came concerning him.

But at this point we must say a word about the character of the Gospels. They are not biographies as we know the meaning of that term. They do not purport to be objective accounts of the course of this amazing man's career, from birth to death. Rather they are "confessional" material, written from the viewpoint of writers who have been profoundly influenced by his life and teaching. They have already reached conclusions about Jesus and want others to know him, too. This does not mean that we cannot trust the material given to us in the Gospels. Far from it, they give us a first-century account of the impact he made on the lives of many. What we cannot escape as we read the Gospels is the directness of Jesus. His personality comes across. There is a "ring of truth" about the writings as J.B. Phillips so aptly put it. They show his humanness, his growth, his struggles, and the opposition to him, as the popular preacher from Nazareth reveals his identity as stemming from One who sent him to preach the kingdom of God.

Yet, even if Jesus did not directly claim to be "God," the evidence is clear enough to show that his teaching, miracles, and lifestyle confronted people with the divine. Men and women found themselves groping beyond words to describe him. And the death of this unusual preacher from Nazareth did not stem the stories and the arguments. Whatever we might say about the resurrection, "something" happened that turned frightened men into bold disciples, that created the Christian church, that made devout Jews turn their Sabbath from a Saturday to a Sunday, that made the Jews throw the Christians out of their synagogues, and that gave birth to the New Testament. Even today, the story continues of people finding that Jesus Christ is far more than a historical figure. He leaps from the pages of the New Testament, from the testimony of the church, from the testimony of his followers—into the lives of all who seek genuinely his truth.

The rest of the New Testament continues the amazing story of Jesus. The first Christians from the very beginning made startling claims for their leader, taking over terms from Jewish and Greek sources that might resonate meaning for their hearers. Claims are now made of him that approximate to statements made of almighty God. He is called "Lord," a term commonly used of a divine being. Other descriptions reveal the estimate that was given to his significance: Wisdom, Life, the Way, and even the "visible of the Invisible God." Thomas, in the fourth Gospel, falls at the feet of the risen Christ and calls him "My Lord and my God" because the good news of Christianity calls men and women to meet the living God, and this they do when they meet the One who was sent.

At this point we meet what theologians call the "scandal of particularity." That is, Christianity makes the bold claim that Jesus Christ is so incomparable that we meet God fully in him. In this particular man, God is known. This does not mean, of course, that God cannot be known in other faiths. Mainstream Christianity treats other religions with respect and allows that

God can be known, and is known by men and women of non-Christian faiths. We do not deny that in the higher religions of mankind there are glimpses of the divine. But we cannot shift from the conviction that is as old as the New Testament: that God is revealed *fully and finally* in the person of Jesus Christ. We know how infuriating and arrogant such a claim must seem to those who sincerely believe that in their scriptures and in their worship God is found and experienced. But we have to say with Paul as he preached to the adherents of other faiths in Athens: "What you worship but do not know—this is what I now proclaim" (Acts 17:23, NEB). This scandal of particularity we must live with. Christians cannot yield this un-negotiable element in their faith. We believe that the God of the universe longs to reveal himself and he does so in many different ways and forms, through religion, through reason, art, and human intelligence, but each and every one of these ways is limited. Only in a personal relationship with the living God experienced in Jesus Christ can he be known.

10

What Kind of Response?

BISHOP EDWARD BARNES, ONCE A FAMOUS MATHEMATICIAN and Bishop of Birmingham, concluded his Gifford Lectures with these words: "I too have realized how vast is our ignorance of the world in which we find ourselves and to which we belong. Can it be, I am compelled to ask, that with such a feeling of ignorance I shall pass to a realm where knowledge is not, because consciousness has ceased? Must we allow that the desire to understand God's works and ways, which is one of the strongest and purest of human passions, is a vain and hopeless by-product of man's search for material comfort? Do we but rise for a moment above the waters of unconsciousness and, after a brief glance around, sink again to eternal oblivion? If such is indeed our fate, then surely the mystery of human life is unfathomable; unreason must sit enthroned above meaningless chance. Now I for one cannot believe that within a few years my brief attempt to understand the universe will have ceased."

Dr. Barnes's conviction is, of course, shared by this writer and by many millions of thinking Christians and adherents of other faiths. And this conviction comes, as Dr. Barnes makes clear, in spite of the fact that we are ignorant about so much of the universe, the world, human nature, and God himself. The vastness of our ignorance does not paralyze our endeavors to know, neither does it make us lose confidence in the comparatively little we do know. The question that remains is: Do we know enough for us to place our confidence in the Christian faith?

Before we tackle that question directly a number of other matters should be cleared out of the way. First, the Christian explanation of life does not necessarily replace other ways of looking at the world. That is to say, a scientist is not forced to abandon a scientific way of considering the objective realities all around. Neither for that matter is the artist or the businessperson forced to adopt a completely different world view once he has become a Christian. The search for truth in a thoroughly disinterested way is, I want to insist, at the very heart of a Christian faith, which claims Jesus Christ to be the Way, the Truth, and the Life. If he is the Truth, then no mature Christian will want to stand in the way of scientific investigation. Indeed, true faith and true knowledge walk arm in arm toward the goal of total knowledge. What this suggests is that life has many different layers that contribute toward the Christian idea of reality. It is when one of these is seen as the exclusive vehicle of knowledge that error and distortion set in. There was, for example, the regrettable error of the Roman Catholic church in the seventeenth century when it demanded from Galileo a retraction of his thesis that the earth revolves around the sun. Galileo did so reluctantly because his life was threatened although we understand that he muttered just loud enough for his friends to hear: "The earth goes around the sun, just the same!" Similarly, in the last century the church in this land made a fool of itself by attacking the theory of evolution because it mistakenly believed that the Genesis account was a literal account. Today, the hypothesis of evolution is accepted readily by most of us, Christians as well as non-Christians.

But it is not only Christians who lapse into a one-dimensional view of the world. In philosophy, the idea associated with A.J. Ayer that we can only really know things that are appropriated by our senses is an outdated theory because this is palpably not the case. How deficient human life would be if this became the touchstone of reality, but as we are aware such a perception only covers the peripheral aspects of life. And, no doubt, we can all think of other examples of a rigid attitude to life, reality, and knowledge, which by ignoring other aspects represents a distorted view of knowledge. No, such unbalanced emphases fail to make sense of the wholeness of life. And it is this element of wholeness that is a feature of a balanced Christianity when faith in God has for them made sense of the data they work with daily. Somehow an awareness of a personal and loving God has become a unitive factor in their knowledge and scientific study.

Second, we must say something about "needing God." It is sometimes said that the presence of religion in the world—which even the most jaundiced agnostic will admit to be extremely prevalent in human history and shows no sign of diminishing—is merely a psychological crutch that reassures insecure people that they are not alone. This way of explaining religion, which started with Feuerbach, journeyed into Marxism, was continued by Freud, and has become folklore with some sophisticates, should be dismissed by all thinking people. To be sure, there will always be those who will need crutches, and a faith supplies this for some. But for the vast majority of Christians such a suggestion is an insult and an inadequate explanation for the presence of faith in God.

On the contrary, a number of things can be said about need. We can say with Philip Toynbee, the journalist, for example, that "It is true that the need is no proof that God exists; but it is at least a suggestive and interesting element in many people's composition. Strange creatures, if we felt so strong a need for something which was never there." Of course, we must not push this too far because not everyone feels the urge to worship or that it is necessary to postulate the existence of a Being beyond them. Nevertheless, the idea expressed so beautifully in Ecclesiastes 3:11 that "Thou hast set eternity in man's heart" captures something of our restless drive for a divinity that eludes us. The presence of religion since the beginning of time—indeed, some would argue that it is the thing that makes humankind distinctively human—is a factor that cannot easily be brushed aside. And that was Toynbee's point, that the universal striving for "something" beyond us cannot simply be explained by appealing to wish fulfillment.

Furthermore, when we use the word "need," we inevitably give it a narrow meaning of "hunger for God." We find it difficult ever to imagine ourselves saying as some Christians do, "I reached rock bottom, my life was falling apart, and Jesus rescued me. I felt suicidal and he was there to help." And, perhaps, we find ourselves thinking, "That's fine for you, but what a neurotic mess you were in the first place! That's not for me!" Men, especially, are prone to despise anything that they think is "weak." Now it is true that God meets that kind of need. Many have found God at points of crises in their lives when God stepped in at the nick of time. But not all Christians find their way to faith through that kind of need. I did not, and I suspect that the majority do not. We need to give breadth to the idea of "needing God." The kind of breadth I have in mind is caught so well in Augustine's famous saying: "Our hearts are restless until they rest in thee." That is to say, that at the heart of every human self some form of encounter with God is required that is akin to "coming home," "finding oneself," to becoming fully what we are. And the ways into this center are so varied and diverse that we can only pick out some of the more popular pathways.

There is the God who makes intellectual sense for us and who becomes the center of our way of looking at life. For many, the Christian way is not the meeting of an emotional need, but a wonderful way of seeing the world through companionship with the Maker. So the poet and writer George MacDonald spoke so revealingly about water: "Is oxygen and hydrogen the divine idea of Water? God put the two together only that man might separate and find them out? He allows his child to pull his toys to pieces; but were they made that he might pull us to pieces? . . . Find for us what is in the constitution of the two gases, makes them fit and capable to be thus honoured in forming the lovely thing, and you will give us a revelation about more than water, namely about the God who makes oxygen and hydrogen. There is no water in oxygen, no water in hydrogen; it comes bubbling fresh from the imagination of the living God, rushing from the great white throne of the glacier . . . Let him who would know the truth of the Maker, become sorely athirst and drink of the brook by the way—then lift up his heart—not at that moment to the Maker of oxygen and hydrogen, but to the Inventor and Mediator of thirst and water, that man might foresee a little his soul might find in God." Such beautiful words express the poetry of science, which is lost once we strip the divine from life.

Then there are those whose need of God has come through the transformation of life. Finding God has led to a total reordering of mind, emotions, and body in which true "wholeness" has come. They felt quite integrated as people before but now, *all* is well. Somehow the missing link has been found, uniting all the diverse parts of their personality and experience. I can think of a senior scientist in one of our leading universities whose discovery of the Christian faith revolutionized his emotional life, thus freeing a rigid and somewhat cold personality, resulting not only in the deepening of his personal relationships but also leading to a love of music and art.

Finally, there are those for whom faith has come through its effect on other people—friends, family, or acquaintances. So impressed have they been that they themselves have traveled towards God. For them, "need" describes what they were missing before. "I had no idea," they might say, "that Christianity could give me such joy or such peace. What I glimpsed through my friend's testimony, I have discovered for myself and what a difference it makes!" What I am saying then is that, in such ways, our need of God comes not simply through psychological need, but through an awareness that without God we have not reached our true stature and destiny. Like most discoveries we only discover what the treasure really is when we find it. That is why those outside the circle always find it so hard to understand what it is that insiders talk about because as yet they cannot share those concerns. Once in, we find the reality that has eluded us—the reality for which we have been searching for years.

The third thing that needs to be said about need is that we must refute the idea that those who need God are somehow inadequate people. No doubt some of us are—whether we are Christians or not. None of us can claim to have advanced to full maturity, or complete humanity, and we would no doubt approve of Charles Spurgeon's wry comment about a man in his congregation: "We all thought our brother was perfect until he told us so!" However, there are a surprising number of people who are not only convinced Christians but are also professional people in society, serving as doctors, teachers, solicitors, scientists, lecturers, government leaders, and so on. Not only is this so, but we expect, and often find, that the reality of faith is reflected in changed lives. Any experienced minister will look for signs of God's blessing in a person's life and will find it if faith is genuine. We expect that person to be different. We expect people to grow as persons, to become more mature, more self-reliant and able to cope with life's problems. The tree is undoubtedly known by its fruits, but the tree has to be there to begin with.

And this last point gets to the heart of what Christian faith is all about. It is not a kind of armor that protects inadequate and scared people who have no resources of their own. It is a way of life that is given by God and that makes us the kind of people God wants us to be. An illustration of the illusions some people have about the Christian life is reflected in a letter written by a man to the theologian Dr. J.S. Whale some years ago: "I am 65 years of age, retired after an active life and very happy. My wife is six months younger than me. We have been married forty years very happily. We have never attended church. We have never said a prayer. We neither believe in life after death. We believe in making this world better. Without being egotistical I believe that we have succeeded. We are highly respected by our neighbours, we are not hampered by any creeds but stare life squarely in the face. You might in your talks tell me what religion has to offer us."

I have no idea how Dr. Whale replied, but essentially here is a self-satisfied man who has already made up his mind that he does not need God. No one would deny his good life, but he does not consider it possible that he could be better, that conceivably he might learn something from a faith tested by millions down the centuries, that he could be wrong! I would guess that for such a man the challenge of Christianity will not come, to begin with, in addition but in subtraction; his pride and self-sufficiency must yield before the claims of almighty God. He must see himself not as superior to Christians he knows, or religious systems he despises, but alongside Jesus Christ. Once there he will begin to see himself in a different light and begin to discover that what he lacks is not a collection of moral qualities but a relationship to a person.

I am persuaded that what modern people need above all else is an holistic approach to life. Have you noticed the tendency for us to add things on? "It'll be nice to have a bit of religion," we think, and so we start going to church occasionally or we read something uplifting. The mental attitude appears to be politics plus religion, or music plus religion, or science plus religion, and by adding things we still subconsciously separate these disciplines into different worlds. But without God there is no wonder, no science, no music, no beauty, no space, and no art. It is not a question of adding faith on to what is there but, rather, allowing faith to transform what is already there, letting it transfuse and irradiate what are God's gifts to us.

Once we begin to see our "need" in terms of wholeness, we begin to approach the issue of Christianity in a wholly new way and see it in terms of completion rather than inadequacy. But here, perhaps, Christianity poses its greatest challenge to us because it demands that we get off the fence and do something about it. We can no longer consider God a thing to argue about rather than Someone to follow and obey. The reason for this assumption is that Western culture has been unduly influenced by the Greek tradition of knowledge rather than the Hebraic way of obedience. The Greek tradition emphasizes the process of argument by way of deduction and induction, the sifting of the data, and the careful examination of criteria that helps us to arrive at whether God exists or not. Such a process of inquiry at heart is costless; God is yet another object out there who becomes for a short while a subject of examination. Even Christian theology is often guilty of this way of working in its assumption that by conceptual thought God can be known. Now the Greek tradition has a very honorable place in our culture and we are glad of it; much of our science and knowledge would be impossible without this approach. But it is a most inadequate way of knowing God because God is not an object within human knowledge; he is essentially the whole of knowledge. That is to say, he does not exist *out there* waiting to be discovered—although that may seem to be the way we find him—but *we exist in him* and discover that all along we have touched and handled him. So St. Paul, preaching to the Greeks in Athens, appeals to one of their own thinkers and recites, "For in him we move and have our being," as a refutation of the folly of proving the existence of the Supreme Being "out there." For St. Paul, the truth lay rather in God's call and appeal to us to find and know him. The Latin tag "Deus cognitus, Deus nullus" (Known God, no God) conveys a real truth. Once we think we have God buttoned up, we are in danger of losing him completely because our tidy systems of thought cannot confine him to the measure of human definitions.

Such an admission may alarm some Christians. "Surely," they will exclaim, "we can find and know God? Isn't that what Christ came to do?" Of course, and I identify with that position gladly and fully. But even in Christ we do not in this life know all there is to know, and the moment any theological system claims to be definitive we stand in danger of losing what we possess.

Then is there a better way? There is, I submit, and it is to be found in what we might call the "Hebraic tradition" of finding God. Within that tradition, which is the tradition of the Old Testament, the emphasis falls not on intellectual inquiry about God but upon following him. That is to say, while the Scriptures are not against intellectual study, they go further in demanding a response to God and promising an encounter with the living God. It is fascinating to observe these two completely different traditions of "knowing God." The Greek way is rather static; it assumes that with our reason we may pierce the mists that separate us from God and he will stand revealed. The Hebraic way is more dynamic, with God taking the initiative. He does not stand there waiting to be revealed by the mind, but he comes to people with moral demands and awaits our response. So the unknown writer of the *Cloud of Unknowing* exclaimed: "By love he may be caught but by thinking never." Such a statement is not an obscurantist brushing aside of thought. It is not true to the general Christian tradition to imply that rigorous intellectual thought is suspect. Indeed, there are many theologians, scholars, and teachers for whom the intellectual approach is an important way of knowing God and I include myself in that number. But we would insist that on its own it is a dead end. God's way, the Christian way, requires our response of faith. He is caught by love.

If then we are more or less convinced that the world is rational, that there is sufficient evidence for us to admit it as the work of a creator, then we are led to ask: "How do I respond? How may I know this God for myself?" To stop here is woefully inadequate. As the theologian John Baillie once laughingly observed: "It is as distressing to the lover to be told that he could not be sure of the existence of his beloved as it is to the devout worshiper to be invited to be content with a merely probable God." Indeed, authentic Christianity does not deal in a merely probable God, but in one who is experienced in Jesus Christ.

At this point we are back to our opening question: Do we know enough to place our confidence in the Christian faith? If we accept the probability of God, we can go on to test the claims of the One who is for many people in this world the image of the living God. For to say God is to say Jesus—not that the person of Christ is identical with God—but that God himself is known through Christ. He is the "human face of God," as John Robinson so fittingly put it. So how do we reply to the person who says: "I really want to find God. How do I set out on the road to him?" We must respond, "First get to know the man Jesus. Study the New Testament. Let go of your prejudices. Let him come to you through your reading. Hear

his challenge as you open your life to his claims. If you claim
to be a decent citizen with no obvious failings or needs,
simply stand alongside the person of Jesus Christ and see how
you compare. Then, having done that, look at the mystery of
his death. Do you not see in it your own death anticipated?
Do you not see as you read the New Testament the conviction
of the writers that in some mysterious way God in Christ
brought you home? Do you not feel the tug of his presence
as you study and meditate? Do you not feel disturbed and
troubled by this mysterious man on the cross?"

But true Christianity calls us to one further action and that
is to follow. Just as there can be no actual swimming until you
take the plunge, there can be no actual believing in God until
we are prepared to follow Christ. A twofold commitment is
involved in this. First of all we must make our own personal
commitment to follow him and that is not easy. We live in a
world that, as I observed at the beginning, ignores spiritual
values, and we feel the drag of this inheritance. To be a
Christian in our society is certainly not an easy option. To live
his values, to take up our cross in the world will bring us into
conflict with those whose lifestyles and beliefs may be totally
alien to Christian standards. Are we prepared to live that kind
of life?

The second commitment calls us to identify with the Christian church. We cannot belong to Christ on our own; it is
impossible to be a Robinson Crusoe Christian. We need the
human family in order to live and grow, and similarly we need
the Christian family to grow up as Christians. It is fashionable
to despise institutional Christianity. "Jesus—yes; the church—

no" was a popular concept among young people some years back. But to say "Jesus" is to say "Yes" also to his friends and that means those who confess his name. There is, of course, a lot wrong with the churches and we must not disguise our weakness and poverty. Nevertheless, over the years I have discovered the other side of the picture also. Sure, there is a lot wrong with the churches because, at heart, they reflect ordinary fallible people like you and me. But I for one am proud of the contribution that the Christian church has made and is making to the store of human knowledge and the welfare of the human family. The fact is that following Jesus *does* make an enormous difference to the way people live and to the sacrifices they make. I am proud to be a practicing Christian because I see firsthand the good work that many do in the church in the name of Christ. I see the hundred and more activities that Christians do for him in the world, and I am thankful that because of him, millions of Christians are attempting to make this world a better place.

This Jesus, we say, is worth following. He is the human face of God. Follow and find him and you will find God.

George Carey was born in 1935 in the East End of London. He was brought up in a non-churchgoing family but discovered the reality of the Christian faith in his late teens. After National Service in the RAF he went to the London College of Divinity to train for the Anglican ministry and subsequently received Bachelor, Master, and Doctoral degrees at London University. He has served on the staff of three theological colleges and for a period of five years was Principal of Trinity Theological College, Bristol. In 1987 he was appointed Bishop of Bath and Wells. Currently he is the 103rd Archbishop of Canterbury. A respected author, he has written seven books on various subjects—Christology, the Church, Ministry, Humanity, and God. He is convinced that often the Church gets in the way of God, and he strives for a warm-hearted, compassionate, and selfless Christianity that will let God be God.

He is happily married to Eileen, who is a great support and friend, and they have four grown-up children who keep them earthed in laughter and normal life.

Bibliography & Suggested Reading

As I explained in the introduction I have departed from the tradition of footnotes. The following books have either been quoted in the chapters or are of particular interest if a reader wishes to pursue his inquiries.

Anderson, N. *The Mystery of the Incarnation*. Hodder and Stoughton, 1978.

Baillie, J. *The Sense of the Presence of God*. Oxford University Press, 1962.

Barrow, J.D. *The World Within the World*. Clarendon Press, 1988.

Bartholomew, D. *God of Chance*. SCM, 1984.

Berger, P. *Facing up to Modernity*. Pelican, 1969.

—. *A Rumour of Angels*. Penguin Books, 1977.

Bowker, J. *The Sense of God*. Clarendon Press, 1973.

Brightman, E.S. *The Problem of God*. Abingdon Press, 1930.

Davies, B. *Thinking About God*. Pelican, 1983.

Davies, P. *God and the New Physics*. Geoffrey Chapman, 1985.

Day, D. *This Jesus*. Inter-Varsity Press, 1983.

Geach, P.T. *God and the Soul*. New York: Schocken Press, 1969.

Geach, P.T. *Providence and Evil*. Cambridge University Press, 1977.

Gregory, R. *The Oxford Companion to the Mind*. Oxford University Press, 1987.

Happold, F.C. *Religious Faith and Twentieth Century Man*. Pelican, 1966.

Hawking, S.W. *A Brief History of Time*. Bantam Press, 1988.

Hick, J. *Evil and the God of Love*. Macmillan Press, 1977.

—. *Existence of God*. Collier Macmillan Press, 1964.

Hoyle, F. *The Intelligent Universe*. Michael Joseph, 1983.

Lamb, C. *Jesus Through Other Eyes*. Latimer Studies 14, Oxford University Press, 1982.

Lee, P. *Why Believe in God?* Becket Publications, Oxford, 1983.

Lonergan, B. *Method in Theology*. Darton, Longman & Todd Ltd., 1972.

Lonergan, B. *Philosophy of God and Theology*. Darton, Longman & Todd Ltd., 1973.

McCormmach, R. *Night Thoughts of a Classical Physicist*. King Penguin, 1982.

Montefiore, H. *The Probability of God*. SCM, 1985.

Neusner, J. *Understanding Jewish Theology*. Ktav Publishing House, New York, 1973.

Nicholl, D. "What Sort of Universe?" *The Tablet*. 2 April 1988 and the two following editions.

O'Collins, G. *Interpreting Jesus*. Geoffrey Chapman, 1983.

O'Donovan, O. *Resurrection and Moral Order*. Inter-Varsity Press, 1986.

O'Hear, A. *Experience, Explanation and Faith*. Routledge, 1984.

Owen, H.P. *The Moral Argument for Christian Theism*. Allen and Unwin, 1965.

Paley, W. *The Works of W. Paley,* vol. iv: *Natural Theology*. Oxford University Press, 1938.

Pittenger, N. *Picturing God*. SCM, 1982.

Pittenger, N. *Process Thought and Christian Faith*. J. Nisbet and Co., 1968.

Ratzsch, Del, *Philosophy of Science*. IVP, 1986.

Rookmaaker, H.R. *Modern Art and the Death of a Culture*. Inter-Varsity Press, 1970.

Roszak, T. *The Making of a Counter Culture*. Faber and Faber, 1970.

Schillebeeckx. *Jesus in Our Western Culture*. SCM, 1986.

Schilling, S. Paul. *God in an Age of Unbelief*. Abingdon Press, 1969.

Sutherland, S. *Faith and Ambiguity*. SCM, 1984.

Swinburne, R. "The Argument for Design," *Philosophy*, 43, 1968.

—. *The Existence of God*. Clarendon Press, 1979.

Torrance, T. *Time, Space and Incarnation*. Oxford University Press, 1969.

Vardy, P. *God of Our Fathers?* Darton, Longman & Todd Ltd., 1987.

Ward, B. *Faith and Freedom.* Hamish Hamilton, 1954.

—. *The Home of Man.* The Scientific Book Club, 1970.

Ward, K. *Rational Theology and the Creativity of God.* Blackwell, 1982.

Weinberg, S. *The First Three Minutes. New York: Basic Books, 1977.*